to a Family's Best Friend

Lassie's Guide
to a Family's Best Friend

Building the
Bond of Love Between Dog
and Family

Ace Collins

Golden Books
NEW YORK

Golden Books®

888 Seventh Avenue
New York, NY 10106

Copyright © 1998 by Golden Books Publishing Co., Inc.
All rights reserved, including the right of reproduction
in whole or in part in any form.
Golden Books and colophon are trademarks of Golden Books Publishing Co., Inc.

The trademark "Lassie" is registered to Golden Books Publishing
Company, Inc. in the United States Patent and Trademark Office and in
other countries.

Designed by Gwen Petruska Gürkan
Lassie grooming and training photographs by Blake Little.

Manufactured in the United States of America

10 9 8 7 6 5 4 3 2 1

Library of Congress Cataloging-in-Publication Data
Collins, Ace.
    Lassie's guide to a family's best friend : building the bond of love
between dog and family / Ace Collins.
        p.   cm.
      ISBN 0-307-44074-5 (pbk. : alk. paper)
      1. Dogs.   2. Lassie (Dog)   3. Lassie (Fictitious character)
I. Title.
SF427.C64   1998
636.088'7—DC21   98-14972
                                                                      CIP

*T*o the late Rudd Weatherwax and his son Robert,
for their talent, love of dogs, dedication, and desire to make Lassie
a role model for both canines and people.
I deeply appreciate everything their work has meant to my family.

Contents

Foreword

*A*ny family can own a dog. Any family can feed a dog. Any family can name a dog. But only those families who are willing to give their time and love can truly make their dog a part of their family.

This book is centered on the ways to make your dog a part of your family's daily life. The Lassie method, which my father, Rudd Weatherwax, used and passed on to me, is more than a training and care system, it is a hands-on experience that allows a family to receive more by giving more.

For more than five decades I have been honored because Lassie has been my family's dog. The eight generations of wonderful collies who have become Lassie have been more to me than movie or television stars; they have helped raise me and my children, and have taught all of us rich lessons in devotion, selfless love, giving, patience, and courage. I have never known a man or woman who has been as true, honest, and steadfast as these dogs have been to our family. If we could all have the character that seems to have been bred into the generations of Lassies, then the world would really be a better place for our children.

I will never be able to describe what the Lassie legacy has come to mean to the Weatherwaxes. Nothing on this earth gives me more pride than introducing Lassie to a group of children and watching their faces light up. I am forever humbled that the character my father's dog, Pal, first brought to life in a motion picture has come to stand for what solid training and love can accomplish.

In these pages you will discover that Lassie is not unique. As a matter of fact, your dog can bring just as much to your family's life as Lassie has brought to mine. If you use the same time-tested principles and guidelines first employed by my father more than seventy years ago, then add your family's love, your dog will bring Lassie's devotion, loyalty, and love to your home. In the process you will discover that a well-trained dog is a teacher as well as a comforter, a guide as well as a servant, a best friend as well as a brother. Having a dog as a vital part of your family will greatly enhance each day of your lives.

I encourage you to use this book not only for the sake of your dog but for the sake of your children. I have found that a child who grows up knowing, loving, and being responsible for a dog has a much better chance of finding happiness with people, too. When your child teaches your dog his basic obedience training, your dog will be teaching your child basic training for success in relationships and life.

I am glad you have the chance to use my father's wisdom, which he so graciously handed down to me. I am honored that the Weatherwax name is linked to something that represents the ideal in the dog world. But most of all I am thrilled because Lassie is by my side each day and night, and what he represents on the screen can now be fully realized in your family's dog.

—Robert Weatherwax

Chapter 1

Lassie's Wonderful Life

L assie. The name is magic. The image is immediate. The legacy is legendary. There has never been an animal star like Lassie, and there probably will never be another. But more important than the dog's star quality or his incredible staying power is what Lassie represents. This canine is no superhero, no elaborate mix of fantasy and special effects, no cartoon representation of something that no dog has ever been or could ever become. Rather, Lassie has always been a real dog doing things a real dog can do. The fact that Lassie represented a family pet developed to his (yes, Lassie has always been a male dog playing a female) full potential endeared him to tens of millions of people. It also made him the role model for what any well-trained dog raised in a loving environment can become. While this image is the way we know and accept Lassie now, the dog who first brought the image to life started out as a far cry from perfection.

The eight-month-old collie puppy named Pal who became the first project of the newly opened Weatherwax Studio Dog Training School in 1941 was not an example of an ideal canine companion. When he was initially brought to veteran motion picture trainer Rudd Weatherwax, the gangly, half-grown dog was loud, ill mannered, and uncontrollable.

As Rudd watched the puppy wander around his backyard, Pal's frustrated owner begged the trainer to housebreak his animal and teach him not to chase cars and motorcycles, jump on everyone who passed by, and chew on everything in the yard. Rudd, who was taking on outside work only to supplement his marginal earnings as a motion picture dog trainer, agreed to give Pal his personal attention and try to fix the dog's problems. Little did Rudd realize that this canine who didn't respond to his own name would soon become the most famous animal in the world.

As Pal's relieved owner drove away, Rudd and his brother Frank began to assess the visiting canine's ability. Initially they questioned why this animal, which had lived with its owner for almost six months, failed to learn even the simplest commands or its own name. Was this collie stupid? Was its attention span that short? Was this the first dog they had ever encountered who couldn't be trained?

As Pal chased the Weatherwax family cat up a tree and roamed from one corner of the yard to the next, sniffing every twig and stone, then rushing at a full gallop and almost knocking Rudd to the ground, the two men could see that the collie was healthy, energetic, friendly, and curious. But when he failed to respond to anything either trainer said, it was also apparent that Pal was totally immersed in his own world. As the dog began to chew on a garden hose, it became clear that the animal lacked discipline, direction, and guidance. Yet for some reason

Rudd Weatherwax was drawn to him. He liked the canine's spunk, heart, and energy. But this was not unusual: Rudd saw potential in every dog he met roaming the street and every pair of sad eyes he encountered on his trips to the pound.

Rudd soon found out that Pal was far from mentally challenged. As a matter of fact, he was one of the brightest dogs he had ever met. Considering that Rudd had been training animals for the movies since 1919, had worked with the likes of Asta from the *Thin Man* series, Daisy from the *Blondie* series, and Cyclone from the fabulously successful *Torchy Blane* dramas, this was quite a compliment. Yet because his owner had never spent any time with Pal, had not given the canine enough attention to bond with him, and had somehow expected him to come magically equipped to be "man's best friend," even Hollywood's best dog man knew he was in for a challenge.

As Rudd later noted, Pal represented what many dogs in America had become: dismissed backyard ornaments. They were not pets or companions. Their owners would feed them, occasionally go out in the yard and pet them, but never really work with them. As they grew from puppies into adult dogs, their boundless energy ceased to be cute, and they acquired annoying habits. Soon their interactions with family members were intrusions, and they got on each other's nerves more than being friends and companions.

This was the case with Pal. His owner grew to hate what he had allowed the puppy to become. Yet rather than try to work with the animal and change his negative behavior, he shut the dog out of more and more of the human world. Bored and left to his devices, Pal became a one-dog wrecking crew and got the attention he craved with loud barking and outrageous behavior, such as madly chasing motorcycles and pulling the neighbor's clean clothes off the line. With Pal's owner either unwilling or ill equipped for the task, it was up to Rudd to reverse this pattern.

3

First, while observing his every move, Rudd allowed Pal to get familiar with his new surroundings. Then, by putting the dog on a "short leash," the trainer began an education process that started with housebreaking, then basic obedience—heel, sit, and stay—and finally the elemental steps to becoming a well-behaved canine. Within just two weeks Pal had developed into a model dog who relished every moment he spent at Rudd's side. Satisfied that he had earned his $10, Rudd decided the collie was ready to go back to his real home.

Rudd had grown used to his charge, however, and hated to give him up. But his job was finished, and it was time to collect his fee. When he called Pal's owner, Rudd discovered that he and his wife had grown used to the peace and quiet of life without a pooch and had decided to get rid of Pal. Rudd could keep him, or they would give him to the city pound. He tried to explain the change in Pal, but nothing would convince the couple that they now possessed a dog they would treasure. If they would come to see firsthand the "miracle" that had occurred, he knew they would eagerly welcome Pal home. They refused to listen, and while it appeared the trainer's work had been for nothing, it turned out that Pal's former owners' decision became the answer to Rudd's prayers.

During his many years of training dogs for motion pictures, Rudd dreamed of developing the next great German shepherd. All the great movie dogs, beginning with Strongheart and continuing through Rin Tin Tin, had been shepherds. It was the only breed that seemed to have a chance at securing leading and major supporting roles in films. So although Rudd loved Pal and continued to train him, the fact that the collie couldn't secure movie work and pay for his keep meant the trainer had to find a new home for the dog.

Rudd knew he didn't have to look far. All his children's friends loved the sable-and-white dog. So did a number of his own buddies. Ultimately a rancher who provided horses for picture work got Pal. Weatherwax believed the collie would be happiest in the open environment of the range, working with cows and horses.

At about the same time, an English-born author found himself on top of the best-seller lists for the first time. Living in Hollywood, the man had written a seemingly modest novel about a boy and his dog for a small Bible publisher. In just weeks the book had taken the literary world by storm. As the author collected his royalty checks, he looked fondly at his tricolored collie. After all, it was this animal that had taken the middle-aged playwright out of obscurity and into the spotlight.

The dog that had inspired Eric Knight's award-winning *Lassie Come-Home* began life as a Christmas present for his wife, Jere. Eric trained the dog, Toots, using both verbal commands and hand signals. By the time she was a year old, Toots had a repertoire of more than fifty different tricks and had charmed a long list of Knight's friends, including the famous movie director Frank Capra.

It was ironic that the pet Knight had given his wife became the writer's constant companion. Although the collie was supposed to be Jere's, from the first day she had arrived at their home, Toots idolized Eric. Sitting by her master's typewriter for hours, taking long morning walks in the California sunshine, riding in Eric's open touring car, the dog was as much a part of Knight's presence as his three-piece suits and hat. Smart, loyal, and devoted, the dog Eric had purchased in his adult years became the image of the animal he had dreamed about as a child.

In 1938, Knight was sent to Yorkshire, England, to write a story about the Depression's effects on the people of rural England. He was shocked to find things in this region had gotten so desperate that men were selling their prize-winning collies to purchase food for their children. As he walked the streets, the stark reality of a countryside without the friendly and familiar barks of precious herding dogs made Yorkshire seem something of a ghost town. For generations these herding dogs had been important possessions. Giving them up had to be wrenching.

Children cried as their pets were hauled away by wealthy dog breeders, and this vision profoundly affected the writer and haunted him during his voyage home. He was still thinking of the children's tears when his own eager dog greeted him as he walked through his yard's gateway. For more than a month Toots had waited each day by the fence. When she finally saw her master, her joy could not be contained.

It was Toots's greeting that inspired Knight to sit down at his typewriter and write a story about an English boy and his loyal collie. "Lassie Come-Home," the tale of a dog that heroically crosses England and Scotland searching for his master, was Knight's way of answering the prayers of scores of English children in Yorkshire.

When the short story "Lassie Come-Home" was printed in *The Saturday Evening Post*, it touched millions of hearts and became one of the most talked about articles in the prestigious magazine's history. Less than a month after the story's publication, the John C. Winston Publishing Company signed Eric to develop it into a novel. Released in 1940, *Lassie Come-Home* (the original title contained a hyphen) achieved the best-seller lists. With five printings in its first six months, the book made Knight a household name.

When Rudd gave the trained Pal away, he had no idea MGM had purchased the motion picture rights for *Lassie Come-Home*. It was only by accident that he heard the movie giant was looking for a collie to play the lead. Rudd raced to his friend's ranch and begged to have his dog back. It took a lot of pleading and $40. As Rudd soon discovered, the puppy he had given his friend and the one who now hopped into his station wagon were two very different dogs.

When Rudd had said good-bye to Pal, the animal was in full coat, groomed, and looking ready for the show ring. When he bought Pal back, the collie's coat was ragged, torn, and thinned by endless weeks spent racing through brambles and briers. Covered with fleas and ticks, unbrushed and unbathed for months, the dog was not in any condition to audition for the job as a stunt dog, much less the lead. Yet Pal was Rudd's only shot. He had no other collies and no other options. Staying up all night, Rudd tried every grooming trick he knew to make the dog beautiful again.

The next afternoon, in spite of all the trainer's work, the casting scouts dismissed Pal without a second glance. Though he was probably the best-trained dog of the more than three hundred who turned out for the audition, the collie's neglected appearance didn't give him the chance to show his stuff.

Back at home, Rudd, now forty dollars poorer, looked into the happy eyes of the dog he had rescued from the underbrush. Even in his current state, Pal was something special. The trainer could sense it more than see it. The months spent without discipline or work had not diminished what he had learned in training. He was still on top of his game. As Rudd put Pal through his paces, the dog remembered every command and trick. Even knowing that Pal had no chance to star in *Lassie Come Home* didn't dim the trainer's affection for him. As he watched Pal stare reverently back at him, he realized he had missed the collie, and he thought the dog had missed him. Even if Pal never made a dime for his business, Rudd vowed to keep the canine as his children's pet.

Though he had more than forty performing dogs at his facility and was sometimes working on as many as three different films at a time, several times a week Rudd continued to put Pal through a basic training regimen. Teaching him more elaborate commands, the trainer worked with the collie just for the personal joy of watching the dog learn. More significant, Pal eagerly toiled for Rudd just to see his smile, feel a gentle touch on his head, and hear praise for a job well done. A strong bond developed between them. Rarely did Rudd go anywhere without Pal. When possible, the collie was by his side from the time he got up in the morning until he went to bed at night.

In early 1942, MGM contracted with the Weatherwax facility to provide and train many of the background animal players on the *Lassie Come Home* set. Even though his favorite dog was not going to perform in front of the camera, Rudd was still grateful for the work. Yet just days into the shooting, when the dog signed to play Lassie refused to work, Rudd stepped forward with a now full-coated Pal. The director, Fred Wilcox, was

impressed and ordered a screen test. Less than a week later, Pal and his master were working before Technicolor cameras in locations throughout California. By 1943, as the film adaptation of Eric Knight's novel broke box-office records, Pal had really become Lassie and had taken his place on the MGM lot as a bona fide star. The collie had a long-term contract, was traveling first class, and was even eating lunch with the likes of Clark Gable and Judy Garland. Most important to the dog, he was constantly working with the master he loved.

Over the course of the next six decades, "Lassie" would become a huge motion picture star, a television icon, and a vibrant symbol of what every dog could be. Treated like royalty during his public appearances, a hero to millions, this collie became one of the best-known images in the world. While each new generation of "Lassie" has been slightly different from the preceding one, each dog possessing his own unique strengths and weaknesses, the training method used to change Pal from an uncivilized nuisance to a model of canine behavior has remained constant. For sixty years the Lassie method has worked like no other.

Without Rudd Weatherwax's patience and guidance, Pal would never have become a well-mannered dog, much less Lassie. Without Rudd's teaching, the canine who emerged as a worldwide superstar would never have been housebroken, much less an actor capable of breaking a million hearts. All it took was a little time, a lot of devotion, and a loving touch to transform a seemingly ignorant beast into an intelligent beauty.

In these pages you will be given an insight into the potential of every dog. You will come to appreciate the intelligence and loyalty you can find in almost every member of the canine species. In this book are the tools, wisdom, and tricks that have made Lassie not only a household name and worldwide star but also a wonderful family pet. As Robert Weatherwax himself recalls, "Before Pal was a movie star, he was my best friend."

Today, eight generations later, Pal's great-great-great-great-great-great-grandson is still Robert Weatherwax's constant companion and best friend.

The dog you buy at a kennel or find at the pound may be large or small, young or old, purebred or a mixed breed, but no matter what, it has the potential to become your best friend. Just as Rudd brought out the wonderful qualities in Pal, you can bring them out in your pet and make your pet a part of your family. This is not a job for everyone; it is a responsibility that some people can't handle. But if you can give just a little time and a lot of love, the return on your investment will change you and your family's lives forever.

Chapter 2

Is Your Family Ready for a Dog?

As you will recall, Rudd Weatherwax was hired in 1941 to do some very basic training of an eight-month-old collie named Pal. Just boarding someone else's dog cost Rudd more than $10 in dog food, but that was only the beginning. When Pal's owner walked away from the responsibility of ownership and "gave" the puppy to Rudd, the costs really began to mount. Before Pal became Lassie and started earning his keep a year later, the dog would make several trips to a veterinarian, eat his way through hundreds of pounds of dog food, and spend hours being bathed, groomed, and trained. Yet even if Pal hadn't won the lead role in MGM's *Lassie Come Home* and become the world's greatest animal star, the money and time that Rudd invested would have paid great dividends in a much different way. As any of Rudd Weatherwax's children will tell you, before this collie was a superstar, he was a very special member of their family and a wonderful pet.

Even though Rudd didn't have to buy Pal, the story of this famous canine proves that there is no such thing as a free dog. There is a host of hidden expenses that come with a pet, so prospective dog owners need to realize that adopting a four-footed best friend is not cheap and is going to be costly in time and effort. In spite of these factors, dog owners are not required to prove they have the money, time, or space to give a dog a wonderful life. You cannot raise a dog on love alone. You need to fulfill the other requirements of responsible dog ownership.

Pal's original owner must have believed his family would love having a dog around the house. As it turned out, they didn't. Like so many millions who buy a puppy each year, the idea of having a dog didn't correspond to the reality of taking care of that dog. Responsible pet owners must look at the big picture before allowing themselves to look into a pair of irresistible brown eyes.

When Eric Knight wrote "Lassie Come-Home," America was still a largely rural nation, and dogs were invaluable to families. They earned their keep by herding livestock, hunting for game, and keeping an eye on property. More than backyard pets, they were an important working member of the family.

Today's world is very different. Most people live in urban areas. Houses are closer together, yards are smaller, and the demands on people's time are greater. Unlike their parents and grandparents, children are often involved in more than just school and play. They have dance classes, sports, gymnastics, and a hundred other choices of organized activities. At home there are the distractions of the television, computer, and video games. Sixty years ago a dog was a necessity in most rural homes, but today a dog is often just another addition to an overcrowded home.

Does this mean the canine has lost its place? Does this mean dogs are no longer important to a family? Have dogs been replaced by computers and video games? In truth, today's children probably need a dog more than any preceding generation. In a world filled with bad news, cold machines, and cruel realities, a friendly, warm puppy can teach lessons that might not be learned anywhere else. It has been proven that children who have dogs as an active part of their families are better students, are less inclined to be involved in drugs, crime, or gangs, and have a much more positive outlook on life. So even in today's crowded and complicated world there is no better family friend than a dog.

But anyone who is thinking of adding a dog to the family must consider the following areas of concern. If these areas are addressed first, then the odds of having a wonderful, loving, meaningful bond between pet and family will be greatly increased. An understanding of what a family must bring to a dog or puppy is initially even more important than what the animal can bring to a family. Remember, if this pet is to be your family's best friend, you must include everyone in your family when you ask the tough questions and begin to formulate your decision about dog ownership. If the dog is to be a bonding link in your family chain, then begin the bond by addressing these three important questions as a group:

Can we afford a dog?
Do we have the time to properly care for a dog?
Do we have the space for a dog?

Financial Concerns

As the first question indicates, you need to look at your financial situation. Dogs are not cheap. You probably aren't going to find a store that will give you food. A veterinarian will not give you free services. A boss or teacher will not give you time off to tend to the animal. A contractor will not freely remodel your home and yard to meet your dog's needs.

You should consider the following questions:

How much can we afford to spend on the initial purchase? How much can we afford for shots, licensing, and normal vet care? How much can we afford for monthly food costs?

The initial cost of purchasing a puppy is usually a very small percent of the owner's investment in the animal over a lifetime. Stretched over a dozen years, the difference in obtaining a free puppy and a registered purebred canine is relatively minor. The real expenses of dog ownership come in food, veterinary fees, and miscellaneous expenditures such as treats, toys, leashes, collars, and grooming aids.

Lassie was originally an unwanted and unregistered dog, and many of Lassie's showbiz canine partners have been found at animal shelters. I am therefore a firm believer that your search for the perfect pet should start at the pound where there are hundreds of wonderful companions begging for a second chance. Many of these dogs will make dependable companions. Chapter 3 discusses what to look for when selecting a dog, but right now we'll look at the cost of obtaining a dog.

Most dogs in a shelter will cost you a nominal fee of between $35 and $75. Most shelter dogs have had a series of shots and have been checked for any birth defects and hereditary disorders, and they come free of fleas and ticks. If it is a puppy, several more rounds of shots will probably be needed until the dog is a year old. Dogs over a year old generally need only an annual round of shots to renew their license and keep them immunized against diseases such as rabies and distemper. If the animal is more than six months old, it has probably already been altered (spayed or neutered) as well, but there is generally a reduced

14

price to alter the dog. The animal shelter can drastically lower your initial investment in a pet.

Just forty years ago most people obtained a free puppy from a friend or neighbor. With the urbanization of America, adopting an offspring of one of Farmer Jones's dogs has become rarer. Still, many puppies are given to families by friends, and frequently these dogs have not been to a vet, have not had any shots, have not been wormed, and come with no guarantees of medical soundness. The cost of adopting one of these "free" animals can run more than $100 in shots and vet fees alone. Still, in most cases, puppies that come from loving homes are wonderful additions to your family. Just remember that they are really not free.

The dog that wanders up to your home, wagging its tail and begging for attention, might make a great pet, but this canine will also need to visit a vet to obtain a license. Even if the animal is healthy, the minimum cost of taking this dog into your family can approach $100.

In today's society, more and more people are turning to professional breeders and pet stores for their dogs. What fuels this trade is a desire to own a popular breed and have an animal with papers to prove it comes from championship lines. It is simple to find out what breed is hot; all you have to do is check out what breeds are featured in movies and on television and have multiple listings in your newspaper's classifieds. While there is nothing wrong with owning a popular breed, many people rush into a fad before thinking about whether the puppy will mesh with their family for a lifetime. There is nothing cuter than a Saint Bernard puppy. As the *Beethoven* movies showed, these dogs are usually lovable, loyal, remarkable pets. But at close to two hundred pounds, the full-grown Saint Bernard is not made for a tiny apartment or a small budget.

Just a few years ago, when Disney released the live-action version of *101 Dalmatians*, the spotted breed leaped onto dogdom's top ten most popular list. Two things happened because of this wave of popularity. The first was a large jump in the price of a dalmatian puppy. The second was the rush by unscrupulous puppy mills and pet stores to cash in on the hot market by breeding and selling as many puppies as they could. The bottom line was that tens of thousands of dalmatian lovers paid exorbitant prices for unsound animals. Many of these dogs were deaf, others became blind, and thousands ended up being placed in shelters or destroyed.

This same kind of thing happened when Rin Tin Tin was a popular star on television two generations ago. The cost of German shepherds skyrocketed, and it took years to fix problems that occurred because of inbreeding and overbreeding of the purebred dogs. In both cases people became caught up in a fad and often purchased without investigating. Please remember to let your brain lead your heart in these matters. If you want to make an impulse purchase, buy an ice cream cone.

When looking for a certain breed of dog, remember that a purebred dog and a registered dog may not be the same thing. Registration means that the American Kennel Club has received documentation which allows them to issue certificates that certify the animal's status as pure. Dogs without registration are purchased with only the guarantee from the seller that the animal is purebred. When paying a high price for a dog, don't be afraid to ask the owner for complete background information, a look at both parents, and a full health report on each puppy. A breeder of solid standing will be more than happy to share such information with you.

The cost of a dog from a breeder can be as low as $50 for a pet stock animal to more than $1,000 for a show stock animal. If you must have a certain breed, a sound puppy deemed unfit for the ring will make just as good a pet as one that has the look of a show ring champion. So before you write a check for the top dog in the litter, you should determine your ultimate purpose for the animal. None of the Lassies have been registered show dogs, but millions of fans have found all of them champions at heart.

Once you find your new pet and write that first check, the real costs begin. The puppy you bring home will need food and veterinary care. You don't need to go blindly into this facet of dog ownership. A trip to a pet-care mart, discount center, feed store, or supermarket can educate you about the costs of feeding a dog. On the back of the sacks and cans are directions on how much to feed according to weight. Obviously a Jack Russell terrier will cost less to feed annually than a Newfoundland. A high-energy breed such as a beagle will usually eat more than a breed the same size but more laid-back.

Another thing to consider is the type of dog food your prospective family member will need. A puppy's nutritional demands are far different from an older dog's. Certain hard-working animals need a higher fat diet than others who get little exercise. We will discuss a dog's nutritional needs at greater length in chapter 4, but for now you can figure your monthly costs based on average-priced food.

The cost of basic health care can be determined by calling veterinarian clinics in your area. Most will give you their fees for shots and licensing over the phone. To learn the total cost, ask about the prices of all booster shots a puppy needs, annual checkup rates, and any monthly pills or vitamins that the doctor prescribes.

Finally, when considering a budget for dog ownership, don't forget to look around your home. Are you planning to buy bedding, bowls, and collars? Will you need to have a run or kennel built outside your home? Will you need to repair old fencing or put up new fencing? Don't forget about the cost of keeping fleas and ticks not only off your dog but out of your house and yard, too.

The bottom line is that owning a dog is almost like adding

another child to your family, so it is best to determine before you find that "perfect" pet what you can spend initially, monthly, and annually.

Caring for a Dog

Once your family has determined that you can afford the cost of a dog, you will need to have an honest discussion about how much time the new pet will take each day. Young children may be eager to volunteer for almost any job, and they should be included in this discussion, but remember that a majority of the work of caring for a dog or puppy will fall on the older children and the adults. Consider this when asking the following questions.

18

Do we have time to feed and water the dog?
Do we have an extra hour each day to spend with the dog?
Do we have the time to properly train the dog?

Adding a puppy or dog to your home requires a great deal from you and your family. A puppy, for example, must be fed several times a day. And if you want the dog to become the kind of family member Lassie represents on the television episodes, then a great deal more time must be invested as well.

If your dog is going to live in your home, then it must be housebroken, a task that is time and labor intensive in the beginning but becomes easier as the puppy grows up. During the first few days and weeks that your new companion is living with you, expect to lose some sleep and give up some of your leisure time. Someone in your family must always be ready to take the animal outside to relieve itself so that it learns this regimen. Everyone in your family will probably be interrupted while engaged in an activity—television, playtime, phone conversations, meals—to make sure the puppy gets the attention it needs.

Is Your Family Ready for a Dog?

Housebreaking alone does not make a dog a full member of your family and a wonderful addition to your home. Your new family member must become well mannered. It takes training to keep a dog from jumping on furniture, chewing up clothing and other articles, stealing food off the table, and climbing all over guests. While most dogs are easily taught and are willing pupils, this training takes time. Family members have to be willing to educate their new dog patiently and lovingly—and make a large commitment to do so.

The other task that can take a great deal of time is grooming. Right now my family has two collies. Lady is a rough-coat collie with a great deal of hair. In order to keep her clean, free of hair balls, and looking beautiful, she must be brushed at least ten minutes each day. On the other hand, Lad, our smooth-coat or shorthaired collie, can be completely brushed in just a couple of minutes. It is not hard to imagine which dog I would rather deal with after a romp in the rain. So the kind of dog you purchase has a great deal to do with how much time daily grooming takes. Make sure your family understands that different kinds and ages of dogs require different degrees of time from the new owners.

Having a dog in the house also means more work in the area of cleanup. Even dogs that are brushed every day shed, and a dog's paws track in dirt and mud. Each family member must be ready to give a bit more time to vacuuming, mopping, and sweeping each week.

I believe the time you spend with your dog is the most important factor in being a good owner. My father grew up in an era where the family dog followed him everywhere, even to the rural schoolhouse. During that time a dog spent hours each day working, hunting, playing, and even sleeping with its master. In a majority of today's homes, the dog stays at the house while everyone else goes out into the world. It is therefore vitally important that the pet get a premium of the time you have at home. Without this involvement, the animal will never be a true part of your family.

Space Considerations

The final area that a family needs to discuss is the amount of space allotted to your dog. The answers to these questions are usually fairly clear-cut.

Will our dog have a yard that is safe and secure and allow it to get enough exercise?
Will our dog have a warm, secure place to sleep and eat?
What kind of dog best fits our home and yard?

A dog needs room to walk, play, and run. Just as important, a dog needs a home in which it will not become bored. Your dog will need activities and ways to relieve its energy in a directed fashion. More often than not, a bored dog is like a bored teenager: It becomes destructive.

Ideally, a dog owner should have a fenced yard. A dog roaming free is not only against the law in most municipalities but is also a danger to itself and others. If you don't have a fence, a dog can be housed in a kennel run or be placed on a chain, but neither of these substitutes is ideal. A dog in a fenced yard can run, explore, play games, and move to its heart's content. Confined by even a long chain or trapped in a cage, the animal usually becomes frustrated and lonely. When this happens, behavioral problems almost always result.

If you introduce a puppy into your backyard, be ready to pay the price. Your new family member will wear paths in your grass, have little respect for your prize plants, find a multitude of things hiding in the dirt that must be dug out, and sleep almost every place except the doghouse. In other words, your new dog will make its mark on your yard. Rarely do puppy owners win the Yard-of-the-Month Award. By the same token, most flowering plants don't wag their tails when they see you or hear your voice. If you prize your carefully manicured and landscaped yard above everything else, perhaps you should rethink getting a puppy or dog.

If you don't have a backyard, dog ownership will require that someone in your home walk your animal at least three times a day. A dog needs exercise and needs to get out into the world. A stir-crazy animal doesn't care if it is raining or snowing; it will want to explore. In order to do so, it will need its owner.

If you do leave your dog in your home while you are gone, there must be space for the animal to get up and move around during the day. Too often canines are locked in a small closet or cage and left for hours at a time. A dog that spends the majority of its life in confinement is rarely happy. It is like being in prison.

For your sake and the animal's, there must always be a place for the dog to eat and obtain water. This special area needs to be easy to reach but also out of the way of lots of traffic. Before you bring a dog into your life, decide where you want to feed it.

Where your dog sleeps is vitally important, too. In the cases of my dogs and Lassie, they chose where they wanted to sleep. Dogs always seem to bond more with one member of the family and sleep in that person's room.

If you want to be a responsible dog owner, then cost, time, and space must be addressed first. Carefully evaluate your budget, free time, and space before inviting a dog into your family. By doing so you will ensure that your puppy will become an important part of your household.

Chapter 3

Choosing the Right Dog for Your Family

When Rudd Weatherwax obtained Pal, the collie that would forever change his life, he was actually looking for a German shepherd. Rudd wanted a shepherd, then commonly called a police dog, because they were easy to train and were the most sought-after breed for motion picture work. When he did not get what he thought he needed and wanted, Rudd was given the best dog he would ever own, his big break in Hollywood, and the answer to all his prayers. The trainer might have been looking for a rose, but he didn't pass on the orchid that came his way.

Like Rudd, most people who are looking for that "perfect" dog for their family have a preconceived idea of what the pet should be. Because of a childhood experience, a television show, a favorite book, or a chance encounter with a neighbor's well-trained pet, dog buying seems to be a largely emotional exercise. Millions of collies have been purchased simply because of the exposure that Lassie gave the breed. In the 1950s the basset hound experienced a rush in trade thanks to a television dog named Cleo. In 1997, due to a Disney movie, Americans went crazy for dalmatians. While the media may fuel much of today's pet trade, picking the perfect dog for your family should have much more to do with your current state of affairs than the glamour of the current Hollywood image.

Different homes and families require different types of dogs. A Newfoundland is one of the most loyal companions you can find, but the fact that it will weigh more than 140 pounds when it is grown means that an apartment or small home is not suited for the animal's needs. A toy breed might be cute and cheap to feed, but it can be easily hurt by rough handling, meaning that this type of dog might not be a fit with small children. Some people have the time to train a puppy, but others might want to consider adopting a full-grown dog. In other words, a responsible pet owner must do his homework, know his family, and fit the situation to the dog, not expect the dog to change to fit the situation.

Puppy or Dog?

Most people prefer a puppy. They initially fall in love with oversized paws, squeaky yips, and abundant energy. Yet for the first few months puppies also require almost constant attention. Owners must make sure that anything worth chewing is out of reach, that they cover every fence hole large enough for a dog to push through, and that they have large quantities of food available. New owners rarely sleep through the night because of the demands of housebreaking, and puppies also require many trips to the vet and several rounds of shots. In other words, they are like babies, infants, and toddlers. They are a lot of trouble and expense.

23

A full-grown dog or older puppy offers some relief from the travails of dealing with an energetic ball of curiosity, but this animal often has a more difficult time bonding with a family. While most become wonderful pets and are far more laid-back than most puppies, a few tend to remain aloof, independent, and somewhat unattached. They may board at your house, but their gaze seems to be in the distance.

If you are thinking about adopting an older dog, remember this: Young or old, puppy or full-grown dog, no canine is past the age of being able to learn. Rudd began Pal's training long after most people usually work with a dog. Pal nevertheless rapidly learned every skill Rudd tossed his way. Robert Weatherwax, Rudd's son and Lassie's current owner and trainer, has obtained dogs that were several years old and had never even had obedience training. In just a few weeks Robert had them performing like veterans on a motion picture set or as part of a live stage show. Just as any adult human can learn throughout life, so can a properly motivated dog.

Should your family adopt a puppy or an adult dog? If you have the time, energy, and desire, look for a puppy. If you don't, then search for that perfect older dog who will come to you with all that puppy excitement used up and replaced by a more mature view of life. But don't become so set on having a certain breed at a certain age that you miss a chance to bring home the perfect dog that just happens to be deficient in one of your requirements. In other words, draw up your plans but be flexible, too.

Male or Female?

If you alter (spay or neuter) your dog, I personally don't think it matters whether you get a male or a female. I also strongly believe that only responsible breeders with a large knowledge of their breed should breed dogs. In other words, most dog owners should act responsibly and alter their pets. So no matter what the sex is of the dog you bring into your life, please strongly consider this option. It will not cause the dog any harm or pain. Your dog will not miss out on anything by not being bred or having puppies if you make the dog an important part of your family.

From the standpoint of intelligence, there is no real difference between the sexes.

If you decide that you want a male dog, be ready for an animal that is commonly a bit larger than a female, has a roving eye, likes to stop every few feet and mark his territory, and eats more food. He is usually more aggressive and stronger, and tends to be more independent as well. By altering a male dog you can affect some of its independent leanings and desire to roam, but in many cases the call of the wild and roaming still capture the heart of many male dogs. The good news is that males shed less.

Most females are a bit more laid-back, tend to be smaller (much smaller in some breeds), and shed more often. Unless they have been altered, female dogs go into heat twice a year, thus attracting the attention of every male dog within a mile. In many breeds the female does not have as colorful or rich a coat and is considered not as attractive as the male. I find that a female often has a softer and more compassionate look in its eye and can be more mothering of children.

Altering a female dog eliminates the process of going into heat, but it may also make your dog a bit lazier. Spayed females tend to need exercise more or they will put on weight. A bonus that seems to be the product of spaying is a much lower rate of breast cancer.

Lassie Is a Boy Dog!

One question that often comes up is "Why has Lassie always been a male dog when the dog Lassie plays in books, movies, and television has almost always been a girl?" Pal's sex was not really an issue. He was what he was. He played Lassie because he was the right dog at the right time. Yet when Rudd began looking for one of Pal's offspring to play the next Lassie, the first to appear on the television series, he chose a male. His reasons for doing so were twofold. The first was a matter of practicality. Male collies shed only once a year, while female collies shed twice. Hence, Lassie's being "off coat" would affect filming only a couple of months instead of much of the year. The second reason was screen impact. An adult male collie is usually about 15 percent larger than a female, and using a larger dog not only makes a more regal appearance on film but also allows casting directors to use an older child to play a younger child.

Unless you are Robert Weatherwax, the choice between male and female matters very little. I have had wonderful dogs of both sexes. Though each has had a unique personality, all have been intelligent, loyal, and beautiful. Unless you have a reason for adopting a certain sex, just look for the dog that best fits your needs.

Purebred or Mutt?

The question is one that only a dog owner can answer. Many folks like a dog with a certain look; others seem to love a dog with the character that only "nonselective" breeding can bring. While there is no right answer, there are right ways to look for both a mixed-breed and a pedigreed pet.

Is there anything wrong with having a mixed-breed dog? No! But the mutt has seemingly fallen out of popularity as society has become more and more influenced by status symbols and wealth. Now people often turn up their noses at anything that doesn't have a long and impressive pedigree and a formal name that contains at least forty-five characters. Where once only the rich drove fine cars and maintained kennels of blue-blooded canines, now everyone seems to try to keep up with not only the Joneses but the Rockefellers. They want a luxury sport utility vehicle and a puppy named Petit Jean's Regal Solemn Judge.

Pure breeding should mean that the dogs of this era are smarter, sounder, and more beautiful than those of the past, causing buyers to lean toward purchasing a purebred dog. But this isn't always the case. While advances in health care and nutrition, coupled with refined breeding techniques, have improved much of the purebred stock, careless overbreeding and the inbreeding of certain breeds may cause some purebreds to be actually less sound than a Heinz 57–variety found at the local pound. While it shouldn't be this way, sometimes purchasing a registered dog can be a bigger risk than picking up a stray. What must be remembered is that in every situation you have to do your homework.

One of the myths of the dog world is that mixed breeds are healthier and smarter than purebred dogs. In truth, a carefully bred dog is almost always healthier than an animal who is an accidental product of two dogs' random meeting in a city park or back alley. A good breeder has improved the odds of a sound offspring by not breeding animals that carry obvious defects. Hence, even as a puppy, this dog's potential in every area from coat to size to health can be accurately predicted. Not so with a mutt.

For those reasons Rudd Weatherwax almost always preferred to purchase and work with purebred animals. He believed that choosing an animal from a well-run kennel took much of the risk out of adopting a pet. He felt that by using reputable breeders he could come closer to determining what the puppy would become based on the tendencies of the parents and the breed.

On the other hand, Rudd was fond of saying that the smartest dog he ever employed in the movies was a mixed breed he had first met at an animal shelter. After training, Corky, a $3 foundling, acted in scores of films, from *Air Force* to *Lassie*

Come Home, stealing the show from every blue blood that dared come onto the set. It seems that in the world of dogs, to every rule there is an exception.

With some education and a little wisdom, almost anyone can spot a potentially good, loyal, loving dog in an animal shelter's pens. There is still risk and it isn't as easy as visiting with a good breeder about his offerings, but it can be just as rewarding. And if you aren't caught up in bragging about the long list of champions in your dog's ancestry, there is also something very satisfying in saving a puppy or dog that is facing almost certain death. You may represent a shelter dog's last chance at life.

Mixed breeds come in every possible shape and size. They can be shorthaired or longhaired, beautiful or homely; they can bear a resemblance to a specific breed or carry a look all their own. It can be hard to gauge what puppies will look like as adults. Every day with a mixed-breed puppy of unknown parentage is like opening a new present. You may discover a dog that shows obvious collie traits, others that have the look of a shepherd or a basset's ears or a hound's drool. Sometimes those looks are even combined in one animal!

Putting the Odds in Your Favor

Taking a trusted neighbor's puppy or discovering that cute dog at the pound takes some of the risk out of finding a mixed breed for your family. Most licensed shelters have veterinarians who thoroughly check out each animal, put dogs to sleep that have extreme physical or psychological problems, immunize dogs placed for adoption, and then alter them in order to end the blight of unwanted pets being abandoned by the tens of thousands each day. Most trusted neighbors also make sure their pets are up-to-date on shots, have been wormed, and come properly socialized.

Some shelter dogs are not strays or dumped animals but pets whose owners were forced to give them up because of illness, death, or a move. Many of these animals are well socialized, healthy, and anxious to please. Many have also been well trained. The shelter authorities will know the history of these dogs and be glad to share it with you. When visiting a shelter, always inquire about dogs who have come from positive environments.

Make Sure Your Dog Comes with Proper Social Skills!

One of the terms I use a great deal is socialization. A puppy or dog that is going to be a wonderful family pet must experience loving hands-on treatment from a very early age. It is hard to bond with an animal that has been out of the human loop for much of its life or, worse, has been physically and verbally abused. A dog that has not been tamed, runs wild with other dogs, and has been allowed to fend for itself often retains its pack mentality. A dog that has been abused may never gain any confidence or trust. While it is not impossible to capture these dogs' hearts, animals that haven't been shown affection, attention, and love by humans often remain aloof for most of their lives. In a sense this lack of nurturing creates a mental illness that is difficult to cure.

The best way to discover the socialization level of a puppy or adult dog is to have your family play with it. If the puppy or dog is eager and outwardly happy, it is likely to have been loved since birth. If the dog is timid, withdrawn, and shy, training and completely bonding with this animal will probably be more difficult. Like humans, dogs all have different personalities, so a shy puppy doesn't come without merit or potential. Often it is just the runt of the litter, though in many cases the runt is the most aggressive due to having to fight for food. It is generally best and easiest to bring a dog into your home that seems as excited to meet you as you are to meet it.

When reviewing puppies of questionable lineage, a rule of thumb for determining its adult size is to check its bone structure. If your requirements call for a small or medium dog, check out the size of a puppy's feet in proportion to the rest of its body. Face it: No matter how cute, a puppy with huge paws has to grow into them.

If you don't have the time to take care of a longhaired dog, study the puppy's coat. Almost all dogs begin life with short hair. Longhaired dogs don't get their full coat until they are several months old. Still, it is possible to make a fairly accurate guess as to coat length based on the thickness and texture of the puppy's hair. If the coat length matters, try to do this.

A puppy's adult appearance is often hard to gauge when dealing with a blue blood, but with a mutt it may be impossible to foresee. The best or worst thing about a mixed-breed puppy is waiting to see if it will be beautiful or just cute. In truth, if you find a good puppy, give it love and plenty of training and guidance, and it won't really matter. It will grow into a winner in your eyes.

What to Stay Away From

There was a time when almost all dogs were mixed breeds. If a farmer or hunter had a working dog who exhibited traits of greatness, he bred that animal to continue the strengths and fulfill his friends' desires to have a dog just like Shep. It is a sad fact that now most mixed breeds are not the result of planning to bring a great dog's genes to the next generation but the result of irresponsible ownership.

While I would never advise against owning a mixed-breed dog—as a child my favorite dog was of questionable heritage—I strongly advise against buying one at a roadside pen or flea market. Because they are usually the result of the random matings of dogs who have received little attention and care, these puppies often carry a greater risk of disease, have numerous parasites, have probably never been to a vet, and have not been properly socialized. I know many of these roadside bargains have made wonderful pets, but many more haven't. It is also my belief that those who purchase puppies from such an outlet support a practice that should be discontinued. Millions of dogs are put to sleep or left to suffer and die on their own each year because of irresponsible people who do not supervise, alter, and take care of their pets. This is indeed a moral crime!

Puppy Mills

Many of the puppies sold at commercial outlets are the product of unhealthy and cruel breeding practices. Referred to as puppy mills, these centers are profit motivated to the point of breeding sick animals, overbreeding, inbreeding, and housing dogs in inhumane conditions. Many of the puppies that come out of this system—hundreds of thousands each year—are physically unfit, unsocialized, and have many mental problems. Their health problems include allergies, unsound bone structure, deafness, and blindness, as well as psychological traumas associated with abuse, malnutrition, and being housed in confined areas. These puppies may look cute in the pet store window, but many eventually are put to sleep because of problems that make it impossible for them to live successfully with a family.

To help eliminate puppy mills, avoid any dog outlet that won't allow you to know or see the complete story of where their dogs come from and the conditions surrounding the dogs' birth and nurturing. Most important, if a situation doesn't feel right, it probably isn't. Ask questions and demand answers. While many pet outlets are run properly and sell only sound dogs, in the opinion of most experts a kennel with a solid reputation and years of experience is the best and only place to purchase a purebred dog.

Purebred Dogs

The American Kennel Club divides registered dogs into the following groups: sporting, hounds, working, herding, terriers,

31

toys, non-sporting, and miscellaneous. Other organizations have added other breakdowns to the mix. Depending on the organization you check with—and there are dozens around the world—purebred breeds number between 140 and 300.

A purebred dog is simply a canine whose lineage can be traced back many generations. A registered purebred means that a group like the AKC has certified this lineage as accurate.

One question that comes up often is whether certification can be faked and registration slips forged. Of course. This points to the need of working with a breeder who has solid references and a long list of satisfied customers, and who takes great care not only in the breeding but also in placing a puppy in a good home. A breeder who shows affection and love to his or her dogs is someone who takes great care in continuing the line. You can find this kind of a breeder through contacts at dog shows, through local veterinarians, and through families who have purchased a dog you like.

A Warning About All Purebred Dogs: Almost all breeds are prone to some genetic defects. Some collies have eye problems. Many German shepherds, golden retrievers, Saint Bernards, and other larger breeds have hip problems. Dalmatians are often deaf. If you decide you want a certain breed, read everything you can on that breed in order to know what to ask about. A good breeder will have already put his puppies through a professional examination and will be able to produce a health certificate. Your extra homework can prevent huge medical bills, a lot of heartache, and a bad experience for everyone in the family.

To learn more about dog breeds, purchase a few dog magazines, go to a field trial to see the dogs in action, speak with some sportsmen, ranchers, farmers, or breeders in your area, or visit your local bookstore or library to find works on the various kinds of canines and their history. *The American Kennel Club's*

Complete Dog Book is a wonderful place to start learning about every breed of recognized dog. There are also many web sites on the Internet devoted to different breeds. Following are the AKC groups:

Sporting

Three of America's most popular breeds, the golden retriever, the Labrador retriever, and the spaniel, can be found in this group. In general these dogs are happy and active animals who make wonderful family pets. They tend to love children and are very trainable.

This group was originally bred for the purpose of finding or retrieving game. Many of these breeds actually point out prey to their masters, and others bring the downed prey back to the hunter.

33

For generations sporting dogs have spent their lives in the service of humans, and because of this they are naturally comfortable at the side of those they love. Families who have little house or yard room should be warned that sporting dogs are high-energy animals. They also like to get out in the open air, can run for hours, and love to explore. If you adopt a sporting dog, be ready to spend a portion of each day on the move.

The character and endurance of this group can best be appreciated in the many and varied ways they serve humans. Not only do these dogs work in the sporting field, but tens of thousands of Labs and golden retrievers are involved with service work for the blind, deaf, and wheelchair-bound.

The AKC recognizes twenty-four different breeds within this group. Each has special strengths and a few weaknesses. Some are very well known; others are obscure.

American water spaniel

Brittany

Chesapeake bay retriever

Clumber spaniel
Cocker spaniel
Curly-coated retriever
English cocker spaniel
English setter
English springer spaniel
Field spaniel
Flat-coated retriever
German shorthaired pointer
German wirehaired pointer
Golden retriever
Gordon setter
Irish setter
Irish water spaniel
Labrador retriever
Pointer
Sussex spaniel
Viszla
Weimaraner
Welsh springer spaniel
Wirehaired pointing griffon

Hounds

When Elvis Presley sang "You Ain't Nothing but a Hound Dog," the lyrics implied worthless cur, not noble lineage. Yet in truth the hound class is one of the oldest and most treasured types of animals found in dogdom. These dogs have raced for kings, hunted with pharaohs, tracked the most illusive game on English meadows, and trailed the FBI's most wanted criminals. Though often portrayed as dull-witted, many rank among the most intelligent in the animal world. Of the breeds that make up this category, almost all are unique in look and purpose.

Imagine a grouping which includes dogs that weigh less than ten pounds and others that are the largest in the world, and you have the hounds. There is something for everyone here. From dachshunds to the Irish wolfhound, these dogs are as diverse in use and need as they are in size and length of coat. The best known of the group is probably the beagle.

Like sporting dogs, these breeds are very active and energetic when asked to perform. Yet many, like the bloodhound and greyhound, are also laid-back and carefree when not on duty. Owning a hound can be very rewarding and interesting. With their loping gait and baying voices, they are often entertaining. Yet many of the individuals within each breed do not mesh well with smaller children or families. If you like the look of a hound, then take the time to get to know a breeder. Most are specialists, and if you explain to them your family's situation and how much room you have, the breeder can be a great aid in guiding you to a dog or puppy that has a good chance of matching your needs.

This brief overview of the hound group cannot be concluded without mentioning the greyhound. Several organizations have been formed to match retired racing greyhounds with families. Research has proven that these former athletes make wonderful pets in both urban and rural homes. Placing a retired greyhound in a loving home saves the dog from being destroyed. To find out who provides this service in your area, contact local dog racing tracks or the ASPCA. You can also obtain more information from organizations such as Greyhound Rescue and Adoption, 8677 S. State Road 243, Cloverdale, IN 46120-9696. Many of these organizations have listings on the Internet, too.

Twenty-two hounds make up this special group, some of the most unusual dogs in the world!

Afghan hound
American foxhound
Basenji
Basset hound
Beagle
Black and tan coonhound
Bloodhound
Borzoi
Dachshund
English foxhound
Greyhound
Harrier
Ibizan hound
Irish wolfhound
Norwegian elkhound
Otter hound
Petit Basset Giffon Vendeen
Pharaoh hound
Rhodesian ridgeback
Saluki
Scottish deerhound
Whippet

Working

Until fairly recently the working group included dogs who were bred to guard sheep, pull sleds, and protect people and property. In 1983 the AKC divided this group into two separate listings: working and herding.

The working part of this classification includes twenty breeds of dogs ranging in size from medium to huge. They include the Alaskan malamute, Great Dane, and Great Pyrenees. Motivated by action and born with a need to earn their keep, these dogs must be trained in order to reach their full potential and be happy.

Although they have held a variety of jobs over the centuries, pulling and guard duty are the two areas where they have been most commonly employed. Strong and often assertive, these dogs are happiest when they have plenty of space.

A breed that has become very popular in movies and with families is the rottweiler. Like most dogs in this classification, the rottweiler can be a good family dog, but many have been bred and trained as guard dogs. I would stay away from making a rottweiler an indoor family pet unless I was prepared to put the dog through a great deal of training and was familiar with the dog's background. A Doberman pinscher can also come with similar problems for use as an indoor family pet.

The working group is by and large a strong group of medium-sized to large dogs. They were bred to have an "attitude," are not shy, and usually bond strongly with only a few people at a time.

Akita
Alaskan malamute
Bernese mountain dog
Boxer
Bullmastiff
Doberman pinscher
Giant schnauzer
Great Dane
Great Pyrenees

Greater Swiss mountain dog
Komondor
Kuvaszok
Mastiff
Newfoundland
Portuguese water dog
Rottweiler
Saint Bernard
Samoyed
Siberian husky
Standard schnauzer

Herding

Many of the herding breeds, Lassie's own collie included, are the stars of the dog world. Because they are bright and have been bred to work around people, many of these breeds have been used in motion pictures and television, as well as in law enforcement, search and rescue, and handicapped services. Most dogs in these breeds are thought of as heroic types.

The basis for many of the breeds go back several thousand years. Because they had been bred to herd, they are usually gentle and patient, and probably bond more easily with family groups than any other type of dog. With only a few exceptions, such as the corgi, these dogs are medium to large in size. Many have long coats. Though some are successful and happy in small homes and apartments, all need to run and explore. Thus it will take some special effort for urban dwellers to give these dogs the time and exercise they need. For most people this effort is worth it.

In the past few years the border collie, a bright, easy-to-train dog of medium build, has become a family favorite, and for good reason. For those wanting the herding instinct without the size of a collie or German shepherd, border collies are a good choice. Families who want to see these dogs in action should make the effort to go to a herding trial. Local livestock associations can usually direct you to one in your area.

Australian cattle dog
Australian shepherd
Bearded collie
Belgian Malinois
Belgian sheepdog
Belgian Tervuren
Border collie
Bouvier des Flandres
Briard
Canaan dog
Collie
German shepherd dog
Old English sheepdog
Puli
Shetland sheepdog
Welsh corgi (Cardigan)
Welsh corgi (Pembroke)

39

Terriers

Generally small, these dogs are outgoing and energetic, but a few of the larger varieties have a reputation for being mean. Pound for pound, the terriers are dogdom's most aggressive animals. The best-known breeds in this classification are the miniature schnauzer, the bull terrier, and the Airedale. Though many people don't realize it, these dogs were bred to hunt game in places where large dogs couldn't be used. Some are very combative; thus it is best to visit with breeders, watch their animals around children, and talk with other dog experts rather than rush a decision about which type of terrier would work best with your family.

Most dogs in this grouping can adapt to any type of living conditions and are easy to care for and extremely loyal. But be careful that your terrier is properly socialized with people and other animals from an early age. If they are not socialized, they usually become very territorial and protective. It is almost impossible to socialize a fully grown dog of any breed, but in particular a terrier.

Airedale terrier
American Staffordshire terrier
Australian terrier
Bedlington terrier
Border terrier
Bull terrier
Cairn terrier
Dandie Dinmont terrier
Fox terrier (smooth)
Fox terrier (wire)
Irish terrier
Kerry blue terrier
Lakeland terrier
Manchester terrier
Miniature bull terrie
Miniature schnauzer
Norfolk terrier
Scottish terrier
Sealyham terrier
Skye terrier
Soft-coated Wheaten terrier
Staffordshire bull terrier
Welsh terrier
West Highland white terrier

Toys

This is by nature a loud group. These dogs seem to be born social and love to bark and yap. Including animals such as the Chihuahua, Pekingese, and Yorkshire terrier, these dogs live much longer than larger breeds and, because of their size and personality, are easy to spoil. As their name suggests, many owners treat them like playthings or house ornaments.

While they make wonderful and loyal pets for adults, they can be a problem when brought into contact with small children. Because these dogs are small, they are generally more fragile. A playing child might be able to climb all over a Labrador retriever, and in many cases the dog will never react, but these smaller dogs will experience pain and feel threatened. A large portion of the minor dog bites treated by doctors are the result of children playing with smaller breeds. All members of your family must be taught to handle a toy breed properly.

41

Affenpinscher
Brussels griffon
Cavalier King Charles spaniel
Chihuahua
Chinese crested
English toy spaniel
Italian greyhound
Japanese chin
Maltese
Manchester terrier
Miniature pinscher
Papillon
Pekingese
Pomeranian
Poodle
Pug
Shih tzu

Silky terrier
Yorkshire terrier

Non-sporting

The breeds placed in this category just don't seem to fit any-where else. Many of them have nothing in common in tempera-ment, appearance, or size. At one time this was just the "catchall" grouping of the dog world. In the past few years the miscellaneous class has taken over that title. Non-sporting dogs include chow chows, dalmatians, and poodles.

The poodle is probably the best-known dog in this group. Though poodles make a great pet for either sex and almost any age group, they are often thought of as a woman's dog. Like the poodle, the always popular Boston terrier is bright and loyal. Others in this category rank anywhere from shy and cute to bold and beautiful.

Two breeds in this group have recently come under a great deal of scrutiny. Dalmatians are high-energy dogs that were originally bred to run and work. Recent overbreeding has caused deafness to appear in many animals. Though most chows are loyal and friendly, this breed has recently been involved in many attacks on children. As with any dog in this group, dalmatians and chows can make wonderful pets, but socialization and careful breeding must be employed to avoid problems. If you are interested in one of these dogs, take your time, investigate the breeders, and get to know the breed well.

The bulldog in this group is not the pitbull terrier, which has been banned in a number of cities and is not an AKC-recognized breed. This bulldog is usually a very good family pet that loves children and shows few signs of unpredictable aggressiveness.

American Eskimo dog
Bichon frise

Boston terrier
Bulldog
Chinese shar-pei
Chow chow
Dalmatian
Finnish spitz
French bulldog
Keeshond
Lhasa apso
Poodle
Schipperke
Shiba inu
Tibetan spaniel
Tibetan terrier

43

Miscellaneous

There are currently only five dog breeds in the miscellaneous class. These dogs are not allowed to compete in "best of show" competitions yet but are recognized in other trials such as obedience work.

The current most popular miscellaneous breed is the Jack Russell terrier, one of the brightest new stars in the animal world. Easy to train, easy to maintain, and cheap to feed, this small breed can offer a family years of love and entertainment. As a matter of fact, Lassie's current full-time traveling companion is a Jack Russell named Melvin.

Anatolian shepherd
Havanese
Italian spinoni
Jack Russell terrier
Lowchen

Non-AKC Breeds

While the AKC recognizes more than 140 breeds, there are scores of other dog lines that are considered purebred by outside groups. The border collie and Jack Russell terrier were recently in this group. The Australian sheepdog is in this group, too.

One of the most famous is the pitbull terrier. The way in which the pitbull has been used and trained—dog fighting— makes the breed a very iffy candidate for any family. Be advised that many municipalities have outlawed the breed, deeming pitbulls too vicious to be kept within city limits.

What Will a Purebred Dog Cost?

The cost of purchasing a purebred dog varies greatly. Some factors that determine price are supply and demand, style, quality of the dog or puppy, location, show ring potential, age, and the breeder's view of market value. A purebred, show-quality animal can cost less than $100 to more than $5,000. In some cases the cost of dogs of identical breeding can vary by huge amounts. In other words, it is risky to go into this venture blind. If you can, take a person with you who knows the breed of dog when you shop.

When looking for a registered dog, beware of deals that seem too good to be true. Good breeders don't conduct fire sales to clean out their stock. If a price seems much too low, then check it out. If you don't know enough about the breed to determine whether the dogs you are looking at are sound, find someone who does. Remember, anyone can claim that his or her puppies or dogs are show stock, but only a few can back up this claim with ribbons, trophies, and certificates. Make breeders back up their claims. Those who are reputable will be proud to show you the rewards of their hard work.

How much will a mixed breed cost? A simple phone call before your trip to a shelter should give you all the information you need. While I cannot give you the specifics for your area, some shelters charge as little as $25 and others have fees that are more than $80 per animal. Usually one price is good for a dog of any age or size. Don't forget: When you bring the dog home from a breeder or a shelter, there will usually be additional vet fees.

As you begin your search in the Yellow Pages and newspaper classifieds, at local breeders and the shelter, keep focused on the fact that you are choosing a family member who will probably be with you for more than a decade. Because this is such a large commitment—a lifetime for the pet—take the time to study each dog, each breeder, and each situation. Don't rush. Wait to find the animal that fits your needs and seems to want to be part of your life. Combine the resources of your heart and mind, and make a decision that you feel good about. If you have unanswered questions, walk away. If you are not completely sold, wait. If you have reservations, then discuss them and try to work through them. Don't be afraid to start all over again if you have to. It is better to wait months to find the right pet than live for years with the results of a sudden and emotionally charged bad decision.

45

A Final Note from the Real Story of Lassie

At the beginning of this chapter we discussed socialization. Picking a puppy or dog that has been socialized is very important. Once you bring your puppy home, it is vital that you keep the dog in a social environment as well.

In the late 1950s, Lassie II became very ill. Doctors discovered cancer and ordered immediate treatment. The treatment was successful, and Lassie II eventually regained his full health and lived to a ripe old age. Yet during the dog's convalescence, the CBS television show *Lassie* had to continue to shoot episodes.

Because Lassie II was approaching middle age, Rudd Weatherwax had been working with one of the dog's puppies, which had already been targeted to take over the starring role. Yet at the time Lassie II was forced to quit working, Lassie III was not old enough to fill the role. Faced with a possible disaster, Rudd was forced to use one of Lassie II's brothers, Spook.

Spook, named for his timidity, had the look of a Lassie. Handsome and strong, he was a wonderfully playful canine that brought laughs and enjoyment to everyone at the Weatherwax home. Yet because he had been only a family pet, Spook had not been exposed to the noise and activities of the set of a television show, was not used to traveling every day, and was timid around strangers. Having been taught only basic obedience commands, he was not a fully trained movie dog. Rudd knew that this dog was simply not suited to a sound stage. He would be the wrong dog in the wrong spot. Nevertheless, Spook had to become Lassie in order to satisfy millions of fans around the world and fulfill the requirements of a television contract.

It is a testament to the great skills of Rudd Weatherwax that for six months he and Spook pulled it off. No one who watched the show each week guessed just how hard it was to help the dog through each scene. Robert Weatherwax has often said that his father aged ten years filming those twenty episodes with an unprepared dog. It was an experience Rudd never wanted to repeat.

When Lassie III (originally named Baby) came of age, Spook was overjoyed at the chance to stay home. Lassie III stepped in and performed like a pro, doing what he had been trained to do since puppyhood, while Spook didn't miss the television studio at all. The collie spent the rest of his life playing and roaming on the Weatherwax Ranch. This was the environment in which he felt most comfortable. He had been socialized—there is that word again—as a pet, not a television star.

The great lesson to be found in Spook's tale is how important it is to find a pet that has been prepared to enter your world. A Great Dane may love you a lot but make everyone in a small apartment miserable. A Chihuahua might make a great pet for Aunt Maude but be frightened of a child's rough play. Rudd was forced by circumstances to bring a dog onto *Lassie* that was not a good fit. A family doesn't have to do that.

The union between your family and your new dog will be a success if you understand what your family needs and how to look for it. Learn the type of dog that fits your family and environment. Make sure the dog has been socialized. Make sure you know how much work you will have to do in order for your new puppy or dog to become a part of your family. Do your homework, do your legwork, take your time, and find the perfect fit.

Chapter 4

Getting Your Home Ready

*A*couple expecting a baby usually purchases a baby bed, diapers, and a changing table. They set up a nursery, attend parenting classes, and read several books on rearing children. Adopting a dog is very much like adding a child, but most people who bring home a puppy or dog begin to think about what they need only after the new family member arrives. Not only do most people not do any preparation or homework; they don't even realize they should.

Many pets are purchased impulsively. Only after the animal is brought home do the new owners rush out to the local discount or grocery store and load a shopping cart with food, toys, and bedding. When it is first brought home, the new puppy or dog has no designated place for sleeping, eating, or playing. The house hasn't been readied, the yard hasn't been checked, and disasters are waiting at every corner. Sometimes the new pet is deemed either too stupid or too much trouble to be a house pet and is relegated to a faraway corner of the backyard, never to bond with any members of its new family.

It takes only a small investment in time and money to get your relationship with your puppy off to a good start. So before you go out and adopt the canine of your dreams, take a few minutes to make sure you are prepared to welcome the pet into your home. Otherwise, your dream dog will create nightmares!

Shopping for the Basics of Dog Care

At first a puppy needs to be confined to a small area so it can be carefully monitored. Yet it also needs to be with its new family so it can bond. If your new dog is to spend most of its life inside, then keeping it with you and yet completely controlled can be a huge challenge. Unless you have a plan of action, the puppy may be sleeping between your feet one minute, and the next he will be in another room chewing on an extension cord and short-circuiting your life.

It is not impossible to bond with a strictly outdoor dog. Many farm and hunting dogs have solid relationships with their masters, but these dogs work with their owners on a regular basis. As families spend more and more time indoors in front of the television, computer, and video games, outdoor activities become less important. This means less time is spent with an outdoor dog. If your dog is to stay outdoors, please invest a portion of each day with him. Otherwise the family and the canine will not have a deep and meaningful relationship, and the dog will be lonely and bored.

For over five decades, first Rudd and then Robert Weatherwax have managed to keep Lassie's puppies and hundreds of other canines supervised while saving their carpets simply by using a baby's playpen. The playpen offers a puppy a place to sleep, play, and roam a bit without getting into trouble. It also gives you a chance to relax, watch television, read a book, do some chores, or talk on the phone without having to keep one eye on the dog. If you don't have a playpen, don't rush out to purchase a new one. A good used one can usually be picked up for just a few dollars at a garage sale or second-hand shop.

If your puppy is very small, a child's plastic swimming pool can be used instead of a playpen. Some of these pools can be found for less than $5, and the walls are high enough to keep smaller-breed puppies from climbing out. The plastic surface is also easy to clean and maintain. A blanket can be used to keep the puppy warm and comfortable.

Another child-rearing tool that will help a great deal with both puppies and dogs is a safety gate. It can be installed in any doorway, hallway, or other area that has two walls closely opposite each other. Usually covered with a wire mesh, an adjustable gate provides a way to confine your dog in a hallway or utility room when you are unable to watch him full-time. The fact that the animal can't roam makes things easier on you and much safer for him.

Like a child, a puppy needs the security of special toys as well. A ball, a hard play bone, or something with your family members' scents on it can serve as a comfort. As you will learn, a toy is a great substitute when your puppy or dog is playing with something he shouldn't have. When choosing toys, remember to put safety first. Pick up the item, squeeze it, and play with it yourself. Can it be torn into tiny pieces that might cause your new puppy to choke? Could it cause injury to the puppy's mouth, eyes, or nose? Use common sense. If you can tear a toy with your fingers, a puppy's sharp teeth will have no problem destroying it. Find something that is durable, large enough not to be ingested, and interesting.

You will also want to purchase a brush and nail clippers for your dog. By now you have probably settled on whether you are going to adopt a longhaired or shorthaired dog, so the type of brush you buy can be linked to that decision. If you are wondering what type of grooming tools are needed for your breed, talk to a vet or a grooming service. You can also learn a great deal by attending a dog show and watching an owner groom a show dog.

While it is true that a puppy or dog can eat out of any kind of container, it is best to purchase specially constructed food and water bowls. Good ones resist stains, are easily washed, are made to be "almost" tip-proof, and cannot be chewed into pieces. Make sure that you buy a food bowl with the future in mind, or you will find yourself going back to the pet store to pick up a bigger one a few months down the road.

Many people have begun to use automatic feeders and waterers for pets. While they are convenient, they pose some potential problems. These feeders are rarely cleaned and therefore can become health hazards to the dog and your family. Rodents and insects have little or no problem gaining access to these feeders. And there are many dogs who won't stop eating when they have had enough, possibly contributing to a weight problem.

Don't Forget About the Food

Just before you go to pick up your new pet, call and check what type of food he has been eating. Down the road you can change the diet as needed, but it is always best to keep your new dog on the same food he had been eating during his transition to your home. An excited dog, combined with a new diet, can lead to illness and big messes.

Dog food comes in three different styles: dry, a combination of moist and dry, and moist or canned. Dry is the easiest and usually the cheapest to use. It can also be left out without spoiling. The type of food your family chooses is really a matter of personal choice. Most dogs will eat dry, semi-moist, and canned. As long as the nutritional needs of your family's pet are met—his level of energy and health will signal this—the type of food you use doesn't really matter.

Designating Dog Zones and What Is in Them

As was mentioned in the last chapter, finding a place where water and food can be served and left out is very important. A corner in a utility room or another low-traffic area is best. Puppies sometimes feel threatened if they are eating where everyone can watch them. Many will rush through their meal, gorging themselves in an unhealthy manner. This can lead to digestion problems as well as behavioral problems based on insecurities. A dog needs to feel that its food and water bowl are secure.

Storing dry dog food can sometimes be a problem. Once a sack has been opened, it tends to spill. A container that seals, such as a small rubber trash can with a fitted lid, can hide the food and help keep it fresh. This type of container also helps to keep insects and rodents, as well as your dog, away from the food supply.

Bedding is largely a matter of personal choice. I have had dogs who didn't like to sleep on carpet; they preferred tile floors. Other dogs would drag a newspaper over to the tile floor and lay on it. Some liked towels, others a real bed, and some just lay down wherever seemed convenient at the time. There are several different kinds of bedding from which to choose, and some even claim they are resistant to fleas. But even if you purchase the best offered, there is no guarantee that your new puppy will find it as appealing as you do. Don't be surprised if your puppy ignores his state-of-the-art doggy mattress for a spot up against a toy box.

Until you are confident that your dog will alert you when he needs to go out, keeping the dog in a confined area where you can always hear him is the best way to guard against unplanned messes. It is probably best to start by placing the playpen beside the bed of a family member. Before you bring

53

your puppy home, decide who is best suited to get up and take him out at night and who has the most room for the playpen. This is where your new family member's nursery should be.

Puppyproofing

The best way to understand the potential hazards and trouble spots that a puppy can find in your home is to put yourself on the dog's level. This means lying on your stomach and surveying each room in your house. When you are flat on the floor, electric cords, cable television leads, speaker wires, phone lines, and other chewable objects jump sharply into focus.

If you have had experience with a toddler, then you realize that the modern world offers a host of new areas that are potentially harmful to a little one. Consider the number of cords running everywhere. Think about objects such as remote controls and cordless phones that can be chewed. What about all the things that can fall off shelves, spill out of cabinets, or come crashing down from a desk or computer table? A puppy is usually much more inventive, curious, and destructive than a small toddler, so puppyproofing can be more of a challenge than childproofing.

More than one puppy's life has been ended by chewing on an extension cord. A number of dog owners have called the cable or phone company only to find that their pet had interrupted their service. The fact is that many of the things we take for granted can hurt or kill a puppy. Some beautiful houseplants are poisonous to pets. Several household cleansers can kill any animal that consumes them. The same is true of antifreeze. The best way to avoid a frantic trip to the vet or an afternoon spent cleaning up a huge mess is to recognize and eliminate areas of concern before the puppy arrives. It may take a few hours, and you may feel a bit stupid crawling around on the floor, but in the long run it will be worth it for your pet and your pocketbook. Use your "dog's-eye view" to

54

defuse bombs before they have a chance to explode.

If you don't know it already, you will find that most puppies are curious and fast. A self-closing outside door that takes just an instant too long to shut represents a challenge to them. They will almost always try to time the opening and closing of the door to make a mad dash to the free world. Sometimes an owner may not even realize that the puppy has escaped until several minutes later. By then the animal could be blocks away or, worse, hit by a car. The speed at which most of these doors close can be adjusted. If you have this kind of door, take the time to learn how to set it to protect your dog.

Check on door latches, too. Many outside doors have settled over the years and don't fully close. A curious puppy leaning up against such a door can easily open it and gain access to the world. Make sure your doors close and latch on their own, or you will be chasing down a runaway at some point.

Once you have made your home safe for your puppy or dog, then it is time to survey your yard. Once again you will have to get low to be able to clearly see places where your pet might be able to squeeze under or between fencing. You will also need to check all of your fence for loose spots. Most wooden privacy fences are put together with a minimum number of nails or staples. Over time the boards become loose due to weathering. A dog who is curious about a smell or sound on the other side of the fence can usually pull or push his way out of the yard if the boards have not been securely anchored in place. The only way to know if your wood fencing is completely secure is to check each board by pushing and pulling from both the top and the bottom.

Chain link or Cyclone fencing is usually more secure than wood, but the wires that hold this type of fencing together can break. When this happens, it creates two areas of potential danger for your pet. One is a hole large enough to allow the puppy to get out of the yard. The second is sharp points on the broken wire that can injure the animal. Fix any trouble spots before your puppy comes home and continue to check on your fence each time you do yard work.

Before a puppy or dog occupies your yard, you have to troubleshoot to find possible danger. Garden hoses, which in the past might have been rolled and tossed behind a hedge, now will probably have to be put in a locked shed. I have seen dogs play tug-of-war with hoses, turning them into fifty-foot chew toys. In a matter of a few minutes, a new garden hose can be reduced to worthless strips of rubber by an energetic canine.

Yard ornaments such as pink flamingos, bird feeders, wind socks, and even lawn furniture are also tempting targets for a curious puppy. If you want to keep these items in good shape, keep them out of your dog's reach until you have the time to train him to respect them.

Another danger for dogs is the swimming pool. While most dogs are naturally good swimmers, some pools don't have a way for a dog to get out of the water easily. Many puppies and even full-grown dogs have climbed onto a deck, jumped or fallen into an aboveground pool, and then were not able to climb out. In order to make sure your pet doesn't become a drowning victim, secure your pool to protect him.

Clotheslines are another backyard trouble spot. Normally dogs don't glance twice at empty cords, but when freshly washed clothes are hung on them, they take on the appearance of a made-to-order dog toy. Shirts flapping in the wind often become very expensive lessons in just how playful and curious a dog can be.

Almost all backyards have gates. It is best to lock these gates when you own a dog. A neighborhood child, a meter reader, or a friend might enter the gate and fail to secure it when he or she leaves. Most unsupervised dogs will see this as an invitation to explore.

After you have found and addressed all the potential trouble spots in your yard, take a second look, this time concentrating on landscaping. If you have a flower bed or a vegetable garden that you want to keep in good shape, you will need to set up a barrier that will prevent your new puppy or dog from getting into it. Puppies love to chew. Do you have low-hanging limbs or new saplings that need to be covered in order to keep sharp little teeth from damaging them?

Finally, most untreated yards have fleas. If your yard has fleas, you probably don't know it, but within minutes of playing in the yard your puppy will be infested. Consult with your veterinarian or the county extension office to find the best way to rid your property of these pests. Over the past few years many environmentally friendly products have been introduced. Find the one that works best in your area and use it. While specialized collars, powders, and sprays offer some protection, the best way to handle this problem is to eliminate the pests at the source.

57

Each yard is different. Each has different hazards. Try to see your yard through a dog's eyes and learn what you need to do to make it not only a safe haven but a wonderful and exciting place for your pet to get to know the world.

Other Necessary Items

During the first few weeks with your dog, there will be spills, mistakes, and messes, so stock up on newspapers, old towels or rags, antibacterial cleansers, and paper towels.

If you are bringing home an adult dog, you will probably need to purchase only one collar and leash. If you are adopting a puppy, you will need several as he grows. For training purposes for both puppies and full-grown dogs, a slip or "choke" chain is the best type of collar. For a puppy a lightweight lead made out of leather or a washable but tough material, such as those used in a show ring, will do for initial training exercises.

If you have chosen a large adult dog, then a leather lead is almost always best. After you have trained your dog to walk on a regular leash, a retractable one might be used for exercising, but these do not work for obedience training.

Many communities require every dog to display a vaccination tag at all times. If your dog is always going to wear a collar, then a good leather one might be in order. This is one item that you shouldn't purchase ahead of time. Wait until you have your dog or puppy, measure his neck, and then purchase a size that will allow him room to grow and breathe.

Remember, slip- or choke-chain collars are meant for training and lead work, not for full-time wear. Many dogs have been killed when their chain collars caught on a fence or on a tree limb when they were jumping. Unsupervised, these collars can become killers.

For safety's sake, it is best to bring your new puppy or dog home in a special crate or cage that is made for traveling. You may be able to borrow one from a friend who has a dog. If not, a crate can be purchased at almost any pet supply store or may be found secondhand at a garage sale. If you are buying one, make sure it is large enough to house your dog when it is full-grown.

Choose a Veterinarian

If you don't know a vet, get to know one now, before you bring your pet home. Forge a relationship and find out what the doctor expects from you and when you should bring your new pet to see the vet. Set up an appointment, check on fees, and find out if there is anything this health professional feels you need to check on before you finalize your purchase.

A Checklist

To ensure that you have everything ready, complete this list before you bring your new dog home.

We have:

____ chosen an area for feeding

____ chosen an area for sleeping

____ established a method of confining the dog to a small area

____ dogproofed the inside of the home

____ dogproofed the yard

____ secured gates and doors

____ established a relationship with a veterinarian

____ bought proper food

____ bought a couple of activity toys

____ conducted safety tours both inside and outside

____ bought collar and leash to begin training

____ purchased or borrowed a traveling crate

59

A Word from the Weatherwax Book of Experience

In 1954 the pilot episode of the *Lassie* series was based on a true story that was adapted to fit the show's premise. An elderly neighbor died, leaving his dog, Lassie, to Jeff Miller. The boy was overjoyed and excited, but the dog had a difficult time with the transition. Lassie missed her old home and master. There was nothing at the new home that was familiar or soothing. The Millers didn't know what Lassie ate, what she was used to doing during the day, what she had been taught, or where she slept. For a while it didn't appear as though the boy and the dog were going to bond. Yet with time and patience from the Millers, Lassie grew to accept and love Jeff and his family. So it is with most families and their pets.

Rarely is the experience of bringing a new puppy or dog into your home all positive. Both you and the dog will make many mistakes. It will take time for your pet to get comfortable with your home and family. Loyalty and love will come only through effort, bonding, and maturity. Yet by properly preparing for the arrival of a dog, the transition period should be easier. The chances of failure will also be greatly reduced, and the rewards will come much more quickly.

Chapter 5

Preparing Your Family

y family has a wonderful cat named Spot. He is an integral part of our household. He watches me work and patrols various rooms searching for crickets or mice, and if he is in a really good mood, he lets me pet him. I love Spot; I am not sure that he loves me.

On the other hand, my dogs show their love for me every time I look at them. When I walk into a room, their tails wag. I know they would rather sit beside me as I write in my office than run around the backyard in the bright sunshine. When I come home, my dogs race up to me. Meanwhile, my cat just looks. I know how devoted Lad and Lady are to me. I think if I forgot to feed Spot for just one day, he would start looking for another home. I have come to realize that no matter how good I am to Spot, he is devoted first and foremost to himself.

The Nature of Dogs and Family

Like all cats, Spot is independent. I accept that. It is the nature of his species. Meanwhile, Lad and Lady are by nature dependent. That is why a dog makes such a wonderful family pet. It is by nature family-oriented.

Wolves and most other wild canines are pack animals. They hunt together, play together, live together, and raise their families together. Many wolves mate for life. When separated from their group, most wild canines become depressed and frantically try to return to the fold. Even domesticated dogs that are turned loose to fend for themselves usually bond with other dogs and form a pack that works together for survival.

If you observe a dog roaming your neighborhood, you will usually find a friend tagging along (unless it is a starving stray). Together they are exploring, playing, and in most cases getting into trouble.

If you watch a dog herding a flock of sheep, you quickly conclude that the dog looks upon the flock as his own. He feels he must care for them and protect them, and he is devoted to them. They are his, and he would lay down his life for them.

Because dogs are social animals, they need the interaction of family and friends to make their lives complete. This social trait is what can make a bond between a dog and a family so very meaningful. The dog's need for love, acceptance, and companionship, combined with a family's nurturing, gives the animal the pack relationship that has driven his ancestors since the beginning of time. By accepting your dog into your pack (family), you are providing him with his most important need.

If you bring a puppy home, feed her, and provide her a place to sleep and a yard to play in, you are giving that dog a life. This might be enough for some pets, but a dog needs more. She needs praise, adoration, and acceptance from you and your family. She needs to be there to greet each family member as he or she comes home. She needs to assure herself that everyone is all right. She needs a pat on the head, a kind word, and a chance to simply be with the family. If she is exiled in a faraway corner, devoid of love and attention, she will become depressed.

One of the most wonderful characteristics of a dog is its ability to wear its emotions on its face. You can look at a dog and tell when it is happy, sad, thinking, or confused. You can read its eyes. You may always wonder what your cat is thinking but never your dog; its expression gives it away. Begging for a love pat with its eyes or pleading for forgiveness with a downturned head, your dog shares with you its heart, so you must do the same for your dog. This is something your family must come to understand—a responsibility that must be accepted—before you can truly make your dog a member of your family.

63

Preparing Children to Handle a Puppy

Any dog is special, but a puppy is unique. No matter the age of the children in your family, each must first understand that a puppy is a baby. It will be fragile, it will need a great deal of rest, and it doesn't come equipped with a complete understanding of the world. Hence, everyone has to play the role of a parent for the new addition.

At first most children do not understand how to even hold a puppy, when to let it go, when to let it sleep, or even when to play with it. To them this new animal is just another toy. If a child somehow mishandles and injures a puppy just once, that puppy may grow fearful of the child. While this fear can usually be overcome with time, the pain that the puppy associates with the child may never go away. Thus a bond of trust has been broken before a bond of love can even be established.

A majority of the problems a child and a new puppy experience come when the child picks up the dog. Many children are so excited by the prospect of having the new member of the family that they can't wait to grab it. If not done properly, this will hurt the puppy, who may then strike back at the child. When the puppy bites, the child usually drops it, thus leading to another injury.

There are a number of ways to prepare a child to handle a new puppy. If your children have never had this experience, begin their puppy care education with a stuffed animal that is about the same size that the puppy will be when you bring it home. Pick up the stuffed animal carefully. Teach your child to lift the stuffed animal gently, with two hands under the body. Make sure the child knows not to pick up the animal by its head, neck, legs, or tail. Most children realize it would hurt a baby to pick it up this way, so emphasize this point. Remind them that a mother and father always pick up a child carefully and that a parent hugs a child gently.

The lesson with the stuffed animal should be done over several days. Make a game of it. Have your child pick the toy up and put it down. Have him take it outside when it "wakes" up. Have him set it aside for rest time. Even have him pet the animal and talk to it as if it were a puppy. This is a great way to teach a child to use a proper tone of voice.

Most children are by nature loud. A puppy, or even a full-grown dog that has just been introduced into your home, will be frightened by loud noises. Using the stuffed animal, teach your children how to use soothing tones. This will serve to calm and reassure your puppy, and it will calm the child and make him more gentle, too. As with every facet of dog ownership, participate with your children. Let your children see you pick up and pet the stuffed animal in the right way. Let your children hear the tone of your voice as you praise the pet. If you buy into this training exercise, they will feel it is important, too!

Once you are satisfied that your child knows the way to hold a pet, it is time to work with the real thing. Contact a friend who has dogs or call the breeder. Arrange a time when your family can visit the home or kennel. Have the dog owner show you and your children how to pick up a live puppy, how to hold it, how to pet it, and how to know when it wants to be put down. Then have each member of your family pick up a puppy. Plan to stay awhile, getting used to the process of picking up, holding, putting down, and playing with a puppy. This hands-on experience will bring about a solid understanding of how a dog responds, and each family member will obtain a new degree of confidence. Think of it as "driver's education" for new dog owners.

Special Rules

Even as your family learns how to hold a puppy, you can teach the few simple rules that will help your dog be a good family member. By teaching these rules ahead of time, you can avoid pitfalls down the road. To emphasize their importance, post them on the refrigerator or the family message board. This is an opportunity for your children to make posters or signs using art material or a home computer. Encourage the kids to be creative as they draw up this important reminder list.

A dog should never be given food off the table. If you want your dog to have the same mealtime as your family, feed him in his own dish at that time. Once your dog starts to receive handouts from the table, trouble begins. He will beg at every meal and even try to sneak food off the table when no one is looking. He will try to climb on your lap. When you have company, he will pester them until he gets what he wants. Not giving food to your dog from the table is a very important rule that must be understood before the dog comes home. Once the rule is broken, your dog will always be hovering around you at mealtime.

It is just best not to share food in any way. We always smile when we see a photograph of a child and a dog sharing an ice cream cone. Yet it shouldn't be done. This is just like eating off the table; it sets a poor precedent. And even though it is unlikely that your child would catch an illness from a dog's lick, the dog might get some germs from the child's mouth that could make it sick.

Even after the meal is over, don't let the dog eat off the dinner plates. If you must give the dog a few scraps, do so in its own bowl. I make a few extra biscuits for my dogs from time to time, and I think special treats are a wonderful reward, but your family needs to understand that your dog isn't the family's garbage disposal. Many kinds of bones can seriously harm a dog; other foods are too rich or too high in fat for its system. A dog will eat practically anything a human does and will learn to love sweets if given a chance. For your dog's health, don't go down this road. Commercial dog food is made to meet a dog's nutritional needs. The best way to convince small children of this fact is to explain that they shouldn't eat the dog's food and the dog shouldn't eat theirs.

Another rule to establish early is that the dog has its own place to sleep, as does everyone else in the family. In most cases dogs do not need to share a bed with a human. For starters, the sheets get dirty a lot faster because the dog doesn't take a bath every day. Besides, both parties will sleep better alone. And a dog that is allowed to get into a bed will probably come to the conclusion that it can sit on furniture, too.

A Special Language

From the second your new arrival comes home, each member of your family must become a teacher. In order for your pupil to learn well, all the teachers must be in sync. It becomes very important, therefore, for you and your children to speak properly to your new pet. You need language that is simple, direct, and consistent.

One of the best ways to learn how to speak to your dog is through a video training film. You can rent these at many video outlets or check them out of the library or tape them off the television, such as the Discovery Channel or Animal Planet, or buy them at pet-care stores. Robert Weatherwax's *The Lassie Dog Training System* is excellent.

Your family needs to speak a common language so that your pet knows what everyone means when it is being addressed. If Mom says *down* when she means *stay*, and Dad says *down* when he means *lie down*, and Bobby says *down* when he doesn't want the dog jumping on him, and Amy says *down* when she wants the dog to get off the bed, the dog is going to be confused about what *down* means. So there needs to be a different word for every necessary command. This takes planning and communication among family members.

There is no one language. Different training methods use different terms. My family uses *stay* when we want one of our dogs to remain in one spot. We use *down* as a command for lying down. We took care of the jumping very early in training with a firm *no*, so we don't need a specific command for that. *Off* is the term we use when ordering Lad or Lady off a bed or out of a chair. We will address language in greater detail later, but the important thing is to have a basic set of commands that every-

67

one uses before the dog arrives in the home. A notebook can be used to list the basic commands and the ones you add later to your doggy dictionary. This is also another fun way to involve your family in the training process.

When to Bring a Dog Home

A puppy or dog is going to be excited by its new home. A family is also going to be excited with its new family member. It is therefore best not to add to the excitement by adopting your new pet at a time when a great deal is going on. If you can, avoid holidays, birthdays, and other festive occasions. The activities will not only overwhelm your puppy or dog but will also take your family's attention away from the job of acclimating the new family member to its home.

It is best to bring your new puppy home over a weekend. When family members are at home and are not pressured to get to bed or get up at a certain time, when they are able to change and adjust schedules, and to participate in the first few days of bonding, you will have a much better chance of housebreaking your new charge, allowing it time to get to know your whole family, and making sure that you have properly prepared your world for the new pet before you have to leave it there by itself.

Just as important, the dog will get to know you under normal conditions, will adapt more quickly, and will be less frightened. There will be plenty of time in the future to introduce your pet to birthday celebrations, holidays, and parties.

A Final Note on the Responsibility of the Family

Before Eric Knight wrote *Lassie Come-Home*, the best-known writer of dog novels was Albert Payson Terhune. His books, beginning with *Lad, a Dog,* have been read by millions since the 1920s and are still popular in libraries throughout the world.

Besides being a best-selling writer, Terhune was a world-renowned collie breeder. His stories were all based on dogs he kept while living on his Sunnybank Farm in Pompton Lakes, New Jersey. When Terhune wrote, "Man cannot see his God, but a dog sees his god every time he looks into his master's eyes," he captured the essence of the great responsibility of dog ownership.

If you are to be your dog's god, be merciful, kind, loving, and compassionate. Give him a world where he can be not only devoted to your family but proud to be part of it as well.

Chapter 6

The Bonding Begins

Most families are very excited when picking out a new puppy and can't wait to bring it home. Yet patience has its rewards, and in the case of a puppy, taking it away from its mother and littermates too soon can be harmful. Eight weeks is as early as any puppy should be adopted. A premature separation from its family denies the pup its necessary socialization process and can be damaging to its later emotional development. If you are obtaining your dog from a caring breeder who works with the pups every day, waiting until the age of three or four months is all right, too. The most important aspect of when to get your puppy relates to the nature of its current home. If it is not interacting with people on a regular basis, then it is best to bring the animal home sooner. Remember, after the age of eight weeks, human socialization is vital.

If you are picking your puppy or full-grown dog from a group of dogs, do so carefully. Don't make a rush decision. Play with all the possible adoptees, observe your children with them, get a feel for their personalities, and try to determine which one fits best with each member of your family. Have a family discussion about which prospect each one likes. Narrow the field, play with the finalists, then come to a group decision.

There are some principles to help you decide which puppy is best for your family. The first thing to look for is the puppy's interest in you. Some dogs love people; others don't fully accept the human tribe. If a puppy doesn't seem to be interested in your family members, move on to the next choice.

Try to see if you or your children frighten any of the puppies. If a puppy scares easily and you have small children, move on to a puppy that shows more courage.

Some dogs are dominant; some are not. A dog that is very assertive and energetic is the kind of pup that Robert Weatherwax looks for as an actor. The dog needs this type of personality and drive in order to be in top form for hours at a time. Yet most families don't want a puppy that is by nature hyperactive. Unless these dogs have constant training, they can be a handful.

By the same token, many families adopt the shiest dog because "it needs them." In truth, very shy dogs are much like very shy people. It takes a great deal of coaxing to get them to come out of their shells. A shy dog is more difficult to train.

Most puppies fall into the middle category between assertive and shy. When studying the pups that fit this mold, look for signs of intelligence. A pup shows its cognitive abilities in much the same way as a child. Is it curious about the world around it? Does it respond to your voice? Does it seem inventive, finding ways to play with you and your children or its littermates? Affirmative answers to these questions indicate intelligence.

If you are looking at a full-grown dog, odds are that you are dealing with a much smaller selection process. Even at a shelter, good prospects are generally found in large numbers among younger dogs. Most families who obtain dogs that are already partially to fully grown are looking at the single animal of a friend or neighbor. The process of playing with the dog, getting to know its personality, and determining its socialization skills, intelligence, and curiosity will help you spot potential pitfalls. An adult dog is a bit harder to bring into a family situation than a puppy because its personality is almost completely formed and it may be set in its ways, so make your decision very carefully. Don't be afraid to visit the dog on several occasions before finally deciding to adopt or pass on it.

72 The Trip Home

Once you have found the perfect puppy or dog for your family, a pet carrier or crate is the safest way to bring it home. Most dogs do not like being put into the crate, but the dog is far less likely to be injured or to soil your car if it is confined. You might want to decide ahead of time where the dog will ride as well as who will sit beside it. This will head off a possible family argument.

If you can't find a crate, then the dog can be held by a family member. Choose someone who is calm and will be gentle with the animal. Since it is probably leaving the only home it has ever known and is being taken into a strange world, the dog will be both excited and frightened. Calm tones and gentle strokes will help it get through this period.

The person holding the pup or sitting beside the crate should have a supply of paper towels ready. Most puppies and some full-grown dogs will get carsick. This doesn't mean it will never be able to ride in a car without becoming ill; the sickness is usually just a result of the excitement of the new experience. Excited tummies are very unpredictable. The dog may also urinate. Once again, this is to be expected.

Housebreaking: The First Step in Training

Once you are home, don't rush the new pup or dog inside the house. The first place your new family member needs to see is the yard (or, for apartment dwellers, the park). This will be your first exercise in housebreaking. Let the puppy or dog explore, but don't allow it to roam very far from you. When in a public place with a dog, always use a leash. When it has done its business, pet the dog, praise it, tell it how smart it is, and then invite it into your house.

Once inside, don't allow family members to hover over the pup or dog. Keep a close eye on it, but let it roam. The dog needs to get to know its new home. If there are certain areas where it will not be allowed, block these off now. From the very first the dog needs to know where she can and cannot go.

During the initial home tour, the most important training element is to have a responsible family member follow the dog and notice when it stops to relieve itself. When this happens, pick up the animal and rush it outside.

When the puppy seems to tire—and puppies do tire easily—put it in a playpen or in a confined area. Make sure the puppy has a dish of water before being penned. Give it a blanket or towel for its bed, let it see new toys, and then allow the pup to rest.

Playpens are wonderful training tools, but a puppy should not be left alone in the playpen for more than four hours. That is about as long as it will sleep at one time until it matures. The second the pup wakes up, take it outside. Don't bring it back in until it has relieved itself. It is best to take a pup to the same spot each time you go out. This helps the pup associate why it has been taken outside. If you continue this practice, within days you will have a housebroken pet.

With housebreaking there will be mistakes, but these will

not be your pup's fault. Youngsters of any species just don't have much control over their bladders. If the pup makes a mess, your family needs to learn from it. Someone wasn't watching it closely enough. Through family members' not watching closely and not responding to the signs and cues, housebreaking will take a long time. By staying on top of things from the first day, housebreaking is not a hard task.

Though it is a nuisance, you can paper-train a dog. If you live in an apartment, don't have a fenced yard, or are going to be gone for periods longer than a few hours at a time, then you will have to undergo this process. Paper-training is much like housebreaking. You line a certain area of your home with several layers of newspapers, and when the puppy wakes up, you take it to this area. When it goes, praise the pup. In time it will learn to relieve itself only on the newspapers.

A puppy needs to eat several times a day. Your vet, the breeder of your pup, or the label on the dog food will help you determine just how often the dog needs to eat and how much food it needs for each stage of growth. After the dog settles into your home, rests a little, and urinates again, introduce it to its food. Watch as the dog eats. When it is finished, take the dog outside. The rule here is that it cannot come back in until it relieves itself.

A puppy should eat on a schedule so that your family can housebreak it quickly. If you find that you are not consistent with the schedule, set an alarm to go off when the animal is supposed to eat. Until you are sure it has control of its bladder and is housebroken, adhere to this schedule. Don't feed it at any other times, remove the food when the dog stops eating, and don't allow it to eat between meals.

How to Address Your Dog

When Robert Weatherwax is getting Lassie ready for a certain scene, he speaks to him in a tone that sets him up for what he is to do. If Lassie is supposed to act happy, then Robert's manner and voice are upbeat. If Lassie must be sad, then Robert speaks in hushed and subdued tones. Dogs of all ages and types respond to the tone of a person's voice. If you are serious and harsh, they will take note. If you are loving and kind, they will understand this as well. Remember this when dealing with your puppy. Fit your tone to the point you are trying to get across.

If your puppy chews on something it shouldn't, starts to urinate in the house, or gets involved in trouble of any kind, scold it. Point your finger at the dog, use a firm tone, and be consistent. *No* is a word a dog can and should learn quickly. *No* should be your universal command for anything the dog is doing that is wrong.

Your dog should have a name from about the time it comes home. Let your family decide on a name together. A vote on the three or four best names is the best way to make this decision. It is best to choose a name that is fairly simple, easy to say, cannot be confused with any other commonly used word or expression, and is either one or two syllables. Longer names can be beautiful, but they are often hard for children to pronounce. They also take longer to say. To help you in this task, there is a list at the end of this book that gives some of the world's most famous and unique dog names.

You need a name for your pup before you begin to train it so that it can learn who it is and what it will be called. Every time you praise your pup, say its name. Every time you want the dog's attention for something positive, say its name. About the only time you shouldn't say its name is when it is in trouble. You don't want your puppy or dog to associate its name with some kind of scolding or punishment. If it does, it might grow shy about coming when called.

The First Few Nights

During its first few nights at your home, the puppy will cry. This is normal. The pup is just a baby; it has always been with its family, surrounded by the comforting sounds of its litter-mates, the familiar smells of its first home, and its mother's warm body. At night, when the lights are out and your house is quiet, the pup will realize it is alone and will be scared.

I have slept many nights with a hand dangling into a play-pen to soothe a crying pup. Something else that often works is turning on a radio or placing a loudly ticking clock beside the playpen. The noise seems to help calm the pup. I also have known puppies who substituted a child's stuffed animal for a sibling. This is perfectly acceptable if the stuffed animal is safe. You have to make sure the puppy cannot chew off things it could swallow, such as eyes and ribbons.

On those first few nights it may seem as if the yipping and howling will never stop. Don't fret; given time, they will. Don't spoil your puppy by allowing a member of your family to either sleep in the playpen with it or hold it in their arms in bed. This will just make the process of learning to sleep through the night that much longer.

The puppy must be taken outside the moment it wakes up;

thus it is vitally important that the person sleeping in the room with the pup be a light sleeper, willing to jump out of bed quickly and rush the pup outside. Soon, as its body grows and matures, the late-night wake-up calls and races to the yard will go away.

During the Day

You shouldn't leave a pup in its playpen for hours on end. When the pup is awake, have a member of your family pick it up, play with it, let it explore, and let it find things that interest it. Most important, make sure everyone spends a great deal of time petting and loving the animal. It needs to get to know every member of the family and have quality time with each person in the household. It needs to get to know the sound of each voice, the feel of each person's hands, and where each person belongs. Your family is the dog's pack, and it is important that it discover the pecking order in that pack.

As the dog gains more freedom, it will find more ways to get in trouble. This is where the word *no* is so important. Yet sometimes a firm *no* is just not enough. Thankfully, there are other ways to get your point across.

Chewing is an important part of a puppy's life. It is going to chew, so the most important thing for it to know is what it can chew on. Do not give the dog an old shoe or sock as a toy. If you do, then every sock and shoe in your house will become fair game in its mind. Talk with your vet about chew toys she thinks are not only safe but good for your puppy's teeth and gums. There are many different varieties of these specialized toys, and you may go through several before you find one your pup likes. This trial-and-error process is far better and less costly than always taking shoes, children's toys, and articles of clothing away from your pup.

If you find your puppy chewing on a shoe, scold it, say *no*, and then take it away and substitute one of its chew toys. Continue to do this until it gets the idea. Dogs don't like to be scolded. They learn to hate the word *no*. If I even raise my voice to my dog Lad, he crawls up to me with his head down, begging to be forgiven. Raised in a loving environment, shown the rules of the home from the beginning, disciplined in a firm but positive way, and, most important, secure in your family's love, your dog will easily adapt to its new home and the rules.

The Tools of Basic Training

I have read scores of books, seen several videos, and watched many trainers work their dogs, and the best trainer I have ever seen is Robert Weatherwax. Like his father, Robert begins a training foundation when a puppy is just a few months old. Many trainers believe a puppy should not begin basic training until the age of six months, but in most cases this is just not true. Once a puppy has left its litter, it can and should begin the learning process. If your new family member is older than eight weeks, it can still learn.

Being a member of a species that bonds in packs and families, it is only natural that your puppy or dog will want to be in the spotlight, to be hugged, and to hear the praise of a happy human voice. During its first few months at your home, everyone in the family should praise the puppy whenever it does anything that even borders on being praiseworthy. This constant praising and the love pats that go with it assure the animal that it is loved and appreciated, and with a foundation of praise it will want to do even more and more to gain positive attention. Love is one of the most important building blocks to help you train.

The other element that will help you is food. Dogs love treats. One of the main reasons not to give your puppy daily treats is so that you can use them as an aid in the learning process. When used in training, a treat is something special that comes with a great deal of praise, allowing your puppy to feel as if it has earned it.

The best treats for training purposes are small, easy to handle, and good for your dog. I recommend dog jerky. It is inexpensive and can be purchased in a large resealable can. You can break it into small pieces to carry in a pocket or fanny pack. Best of all, every dog I have ever met loves jerky.

Love and treats are at the heart of the training recipe, but they must be stirred together with another special tool—kindness.

Albert Payson Terhune, the author and dog trainer, observed the way his dogs responded to his voice; they seemed to understand about one out of every four words he said. How much did they really understand? Who knows? The important thing was that they were able to pick up on the key words in each sentence and the tone in which they were delivered, and then respond to their master appropriately.

79

Watching Robert Weatherwax work with Lassie, one of the first things you notice is the manner in which he speaks. While most dog trainers bark out single-word orders, Robert talks to his dog the way Terhune did. In a kind voice he might say, "Lassie, I want you to sit." Lassie then happily sits on command.

Robert Weatherwax believes in not ordering a dog to respond but in politely requesting him to do something. This asking method serves two purposes: It gives you a chance to use an upbeat voice with your dog, and it allows the dog to be addressed in the same fashion as the other members of your family.

Basic Training Commands

This basic foundation training can involve almost any member of your family who is old enough to walk and talk. Still, the initial lessons should probably be given by an older child or adult who has a great deal of patience and will know when to reward the dog. Also, beginning lessons should be one-on-one. Like any child, a puppy's mind and eyes will wander. The less you give it to concentrate on, the faster it will learn. Try to work with your dog two or three times a day for a total training time of half an hour.

The first command your dog needs to learn is *come. Come* is the foundation for everything that will follow. If your pup does not come when called, then you will be at a loss for every other training task. When your puppy has begun to respond to family members, this command should be easy to master.

To do obedience work properly, the slip-chain collar and leash must be put on correctly. This is really very easy to do, but explanations of the process can be confusing. A lot of people must be given hands-on instruction before they can accomplish it. So if after following these directions you are incorrectly placing the slip-chain around your dog's neck, have your vet, a show dog handler, or a pet-care employee show you how it is done.

First you need to place your dog on your left and have it sit. Drop the chain through one of the two end loops (they are the same size). Notice I said to drop the chain through the loop; don't try to fit the loop through the loop. Done properly, the two loops will meet and the chain will form a circle. If you pull on the outside loop, the chain's circle will grow smaller.

Now slip the circle over your dog's head and slide the collar down to its neck. Attach the leash-locking clasp to the loop you pulled to make the circle smaller. If you have placed the collar on the right way, the chain will tighten from the top. This means that the extra chain will come around the dog's neck and out from the top as it tightens. If you have properly attached the collar, when you release pressure on the leash, the chain will slide back to a relaxed position. Before trying this with your dog, you might want to use a stuffed animal or your own wrist to test the method.

The slip-chain is a necessary part of the training because it gives you the proper control over the dog. If the dog is pulling too much, the chain automatically tightens around its neck, making the animal uncomfortable. If the dog is walking properly, for example, it is rewarded because the chain is relaxed. Though many people do not realize it, this is a much more humane way to train than using a leather collar, which tends to choke the dog and gives the trainer little control.

A chain leash should not be used for training. Chains can cause cuts and bruises on your palms and fingers. You will be pulled by your dog from time to time and must have a firm hold on the leash, so a leather, strong cloth, or canvas leash will feel much better in your hands.

Place the slip-chain collar around the pup's neck. Adjust it so it will tighten around the neck when tugged lightly. Then hook a short, lightweight leash onto the collar at the "pull" point. Initially the puppy will probably fight the collar and leash. This is natural. Remember that the first time you put on a ring, watch, or necklace it took you a while to get used to it. Yet over time your puppy will associate the collar with fun activity and not fight it at all because you will be using both vocal praise and a special treat for accomplishing the task.

To begin, sit your puppy down, then back away to the end of the leash and say something like "Come, Princess. Come to me." Emphasize the key word *come* every time you use it. At that point pull on the leash.

If you do have to pull your puppy to you, do so gently, then praise it and give it a treat. Walk to where the puppy was and ask it to come to you again. Don't be surprised if your puppy learns the *come* command in just a few minutes, but don't be discouraged if it doesn't. For some dogs with short attention spans, it takes a few lessons to learn to come.

Remember that puppies tire easily, so keep the lessons short. If the dog acts bored or restless after only a few minutes, let it go back to doing something it wants to do. Then continue the lesson a few hours later.

Some trainers use a specific hand signal when they teach each command. If you want your puppy to know a "silent" language, have a sign for *come*. I simply make a beckoning motion with my hand, and my dogs come to me. From their early training they associated this with *come*. The silent commands are very useful if your dogs do therapy work in hospitals or nursing homes. You will be able to put your dog through its paces without having to use vocal commands. Any dog can learn hand and vocal commands at the same time.

When your puppy has learned *come* and responds to it every time, you are ready to move on to *sit*. Your training will again be on a lead, so once again place the collar and leash on your

82

HAND SIGNALS, SUCH AS THESE FOR SIT AND DOWN, CAN BE USED IN EVERY SITUATION. A COMBINATION OF HAND AND VOCAL COMMANDS MAKES A DOG BILINGUAL.

pup. Take a position in front of the dog, off-center, just to the dog's right. Make sure it is standing on all four feet. In a friendly tone, invite the dog to sit by saying something like, "Sit, Princess. Will you please sit?" Once again, stress the word *sit*. As you do this, hold the lead with your left hand and place your right hand just above the dog's back legs. Gently push on its back until the dog sits down. When it does, even if you had to help it, praise the pup and give it a treat.

Once your puppy can sit beside you, move to the front and give it the same command. Robert Weatherwax often lifts his hand above his head while asking Lassie to sit. Since *sit* is a command that you might want to use on occasions when talking would be undesirable, couple a signal with your command. Remember to use the same hand signal with the same word for every command. Don't confuse your puppy or dog by giving conflicting or confusing commands to learn. To make sure everyone in the family uses the same signals, add them to your dog dictionary (see page 68).

83

The final basic command is *down*, which you use when you want your puppy to lie down. Begin with your puppy in the sitting position and say, "Down, Princess. I want you to lie down." Then, while holding your right hand over the dog's back legs to keep it sitting, gently pull its front legs out straight and lie the dog down. When it gets to the down position, praise the pup and give it a treat. Because this position is a bit more complicated, it might take a bit longer to learn, but with patience, consistent work, and lots of praise, your pet will learn it.

Come, sit, and *down* are the foundation for *stay,* which you will tackle in the next phase of training. These three commands are essential if you want your puppy to graduate to harder commands, tricks, and tasks. Continue to work on these basic commands each day even after you have graduated to more difficult training tasks.

Bringing in the Family

Housebreaking can include everyone in your family who can walk and talk, but basic training is best handled by the family member who has the strongest teaching talents. Once the family teacher is confident that the pupil knows its lessons, bring everyone else into the process. Let family members watch the puppy perform and have them listen carefully to what is said and done. Then have the teacher instruct and observe as each family member puts the dog through the basic training skills. Sometimes it is hard for young children to understand the use of specific words and a kind voice. Having them learn the right command words and the kind voice when addressing the family dog, and seeing how the dog responds to their kindness, will teach them a lesson about how to treat family and friends, too. In this way the relationship with the family dog becomes a role model for every positive relationship in life.

A Quick Review

In every facet of training there are simple things that your family needs to keep in mind. Knowing the following seven truths of training will allow your family to more quickly develop a dog who can be trusted and made a full part of the family.

1. Begin the training as soon as you bring your pup home.
2. Set a goal of training about fifteen minutes a day, broken into two or three sessions.
3. Give praise, praise, praise, and more praise for everything your puppy does well.
4. Use treats for training only.
5. Be consistent and fair.
6. Remember that your puppy is just a baby; don't demand that it learn too much too fast.
7. Never forget that you cannot express too much love for your dog.

Photographing and Videotaping the Family's Best Friend

Thanks to the *Lassie* movies and television shows, Robert Weatherwax has a full record of each generation of Lassies, but until recently families haven't had this option. It is always rewarding to make an effort to record activities with your dog on film and video. Some of the most precious photos my family has are of our dogs taking part in Easter egg hunts and watching our boys play ball. Like children, puppies grow up in a hurry. Someday your children will want to recall the special times they had with their dog. If you take pictures and record images on video, these moments can be with you forever. Don't miss the opportunities for documenting the special times that a dog brings to your family.

A Special Word to Those Who Have Adopted a Full-Grown Dog

Most of the topics discussed in this chapter concerning a puppy will work for an adult dog. Still, there are a few other things to think about.

Unlike a puppy, the adult dog will probably not need to nap and may want to play after getting to know its home on that first day. It is important that the family begin the process of play in a way that will promote good manners. If the dog isn't going to be allowed on the furniture, then don't play with it there on the first day. It is also wise not to be rowdy inside. Take the dog out into the yard, see if it is interested in a ball or Frisbee, and check out what it wants to do. Initially the dog may just want to explore. Give it time to settle in. When it seems ready to go back inside, let it go in with you. Most important, try to have a family member with the dog at all times during its first few days. It needs to be assured that this is not just a temporary relationship.

If your adult dog is not housebroken already, this should be an easy task. A full-grown dog will have control of its bladder. Take it out as you would a puppy. Once you have established a schedule, it will not need to be taken out in the middle of the night. As with a puppy, it is wise to confine the adult dog to one area of the house until you are confident it knows the rules. A child's safety gate can be used in much the same way as a playpen. Chewing and other destructive behavior can be addressed as with a pup.

The basic training foundation is the same. Most adult dogs will be able to learn *come*, *sit*, and *down* even faster than puppies. A dog that has not been brought up on a slip-chain collar and leash may resist it. Don't give in. Through love, praise, and treats, it will come to learn that putting on the collar means receiving treats, getting to perform, and spending time with its family.

Chapter 7

Daily Care

A LONG-HAIRED DOG LIKE LASSIE SHOULD BE BRUSHED EVERY DAY.

O ne of the best ways to bond with a pet is to be involved in a regular one-on-one activity. Most dogs love to have attention they can depend on. They will look forward to being walked or trained each day. If you start early enough, your dog will also look forward to being brushed and groomed. Almost all these jobs can be family activities. Here is a chance to include everyone in some facet of your dog's daily needs.

Brushing

Almost every dog should be brushed at least three times a week, and some longhaired dogs even more often. Brushing is not as much trouble as many people assume. In fact, once a dog has gotten used to being brushed and knows the routine, almost anyone can do it. Even an elementary-school-age child can learn to properly brush most breeds of dogs.

Many use the excuse that they have a shorthaired dog, such as a bloodhound, so they don't need to brush it. The fact is that every dog needs to be brushed on a regular basis. One of the main reasons a dog scratches itself is to remove dead hair. If you brush the dog several times a week, it won't have to spend hours trying to remove the dead hair itself. If health concerns aren't enough of a reason, the hair of even shorthaired dogs doesn't look good on carpets, beds, and furniture. Brushing your dog is a necessary facet of care.

Besides removing hair, regular brushing also stimulates the glands in a dog's skin. The oil that is released helps prevent the coat from drying out, thus helping to control dry skin, itching, and future shedding.

Brushing cleans a coat between baths. Ultimately, a dog that is brushed often looks, and is, healthier.

Dogs with short, smooth coats are easy to brush. A wire brush, commonly called a slicker, or a comb can do the job in no time. Begin at the head and work toward the back. Be careful not to push the brush too hard or too deep. In addition to brushing, many shorthaired dogs love to have their coats rubbed with a towel or cloth.

Dogs with curly hair are usually professionally clipped and groomed often. In between groomings, these dogs require a medium metal-toothed brush, which has longer teeth than those of a slicker. If you aren't sure of the difference, ask a store employee for help. It is important to be careful when working on the coat of a curly-haired dog. You don't want to catch the brush in a tangled patch and pull the hair out by the roots.

Dogs who have straight medium-length hair can be brushed with a natural or bristle type of brush. As with other coat lengths, start at the dog's head and work toward the rear.

Longhaired dogs require a stiff-wire brush. Before you go to work, remember that almost all of these dogs have soft, downy undercoats, too. To brush the dog well, you have to pull the top coat back with one hand, then brush from the bottom to the top of the hair. This will remove the dead parts of the undercoat and clean the outer coat as well. It will take time, but this type of section-by-section work is required to prevent the tangles, hair balls, and skin infections that can result from a dog's having matted or dirty hair.

Longhaired dogs must be brushed very often. If they are not, the areas around the ears, under the armpits, and on the chest are very prone to tangle. These tangles will not only hold dirt but will constantly pull and tear away from the skin, creating painful open wounds. Often these wounds cannot be seen because they are under so much fur, and left untreated, they can become infected. If your longhaired dog smells bad, it may be due to the fact that your grooming has left tangles which have resulted in collections of dirt or created injuries.

89

The longer and thicker a dog's coat, and the larger the animal, the harder the job of brushing. While a child should be encouraged to help with the task of brushing such a dog, it shouldn't be left entirely up to the child. Make sure that the person in charge of brushing a longhaired dog is capable of doing all the work and seeing to all the possible trouble areas.

There may be areas where the hair is too tangled to brush. When you find a spot like this, first try to use sharp-pointed scissors to poke through the hair and get near the skin; then pull the tangle through the balled-up fur. It may take you several times before you loosen enough of the problem tangle to brush the hair out. If you cannot untangle the hair in this manner, then trim it carefully.

No matter the length of your dog's hair, instruct children to be careful around the dog's ears and eyes. Most brushes have very sharp wire bristles that can cause injury to a dog. A child who is not old enough to brush carefully around these areas can help you with the dog's back or sides, and you can brush the head yourself.

If you want to watch a real professional in action, go to a dog show. In the grooming areas you can see men and women brushing and combing dogs that have a coat just like your dog's. Most dog owners won't mind if you ask a few questions. You might want to take a few notes or even bring a camcorder and film the process. What you learn at a dog show will probably save you a great deal of time and also make the brushing process much easier on your dog.

Nails

If you walk your dog on cement sidewalks or hard pavement, it probably will not need to have its nails trimmed very often. Still, from time to time almost all dogs have to have their nails clipped. I have never known a dog who liked it. Because this process can be trying for both the groomer and the dog, and because possible injury to the dog can occur, I recommend that young children never cut a dog's nails.

You can go three different ways when you purchase a nail trimmer. The cheapest two are the easiest to find. The most common nail clipper looks like a larger version of the ones you may use on yourself. The other inexpensive clipper looks a great deal like scissors. Both work, but I prefer the former because they have a "sighting" line that helps you clip the nail before you hit the quick, or the living part of the nail.

A newer version of dog nail clippers is electrically powered. This style works best, but these clippers may cost $60 or more. Unless you have several dogs, this tool may not be worth the cost.

Long nails hamper a dog's ability to move and in some cases can lead to lameness. So, as you sit down to begin and your dog looks mournfully into your face, remember that you are really doing this for your pet's own good.

I recommend using a small flashlight to help you find where the quick begins. If your dog has light-colored nails, the light will shine through the end of the nails and will show clearly the dark part of the nail that should not be trimmed. If the dog's nails are dark, turn the paw over, shine the light on the underside of the nails, and look for the hollowed region. This is the part that needs to be clipped.

As long as you cut the dead "shell" of the nail, your dog will feel nothing. If you cut too deeply, your dog will quickly let you know you have gone too far. You will also have to deal with some bleeding. Apply some pressure with a cotton swab soaked in cold water to stop the flow of blood. Don't quit if you make a mistake; just be more careful on the other nails.

91

TRIM YOUR
DOG'S NAILS AT
LEAST TWICE A
MONTH, AND
HE WILL GROW
CONFIDENT
IN YOUR
ABILITIES.

After clipping, you can round or smooth your dog's nails with an emery board or file. Most dogs don't mind this. One word of warning: If you cut into the quick on any of the nails, avoid filing them for several days.

You will probably need to trim your dog's nails at least twice a month, and if you cut them often, you will learn not to cut too deeply. Best of all, your dog will grow used to the process. And even though your dog will probably never like it, with time it will at least grow confident in your abilities.

Ears

Ears are another area best left to an adult. The goal here is to keep the ears clean. The best tool to use is a cotton swab coated with a drop of baby oil. Clean just the upper part of the inside of the ear; never go into the ear canal. If this area is very dirty or filled with wax, take your dog to the veterinarian for it to be cleaned. If the extreme top of your dog's ears are dirty, you can use a cotton ball here.

One final word of caution: Be gentle. Most dogs don't mind your cleaning their ears as long as you are careful and don't dig too hard.

92

Teeth

A dog does need to have its teeth attended to from time to time. A yellow or dark plaque buildup above the gums is a sign of real trouble. Since your dog is not able to get false teeth, you should begin brushing its teeth when it is a puppy. Brush its teeth as you would your own. A firm-bristled toothbrush is best, and while there are doggy toothpastes at pet-care shops, your family favorite will work just as well. Make sure you pay special attention to the gum area.

Brush your dog's teeth as often as needed, up to twice a week, to keep them clean and white. Consult your vet if you find any chipped or decaying teeth.

There are also many treats and chew toys available that can help in the cleaning process. Some will work on your dog; others won't. Experiment and see if you can find one that helps prevent plaque buildup.

Bathing

This is one grooming project in which almost every member of the family can participate. There are several reasons that most dogs don't like baths. The first is that they are rarely exposed to bathing; it is not a part of their routine. The second is that they are often bathed in water that is freezing cold or much too hot. The third reason is that they often get stinging soap in their eyes. All three of these problems can easily be addressed. While your dog may never love its bath, it might come to at least tolerate the activity.

Most dogs do not like showers, so it is best to bathe a dog in warm (not hot) water in a tub. Use the leash to control a dog that does not like to be bathed. Since many bathtubs now have handheld shower nozzles, getting a dog wet and then rinsing it off is much easier today than it was just a few years ago.

After you have gotten the dog wet to the skin—and in long-haired dogs with undercoats, this might take quite a bit of time and water—then lather on the shampoo. Use one that has been designed for a dog. These shampoos don't sting a dog's eyes, are gentle on their coat and skin, often help prevent fleas and ticks, and usually leave the dog smelling very nice. If your dog is really dirty, rinse it once, then apply more shampoo and repeat the process. Make sure not to leave any soap in the coat because it can irritate a dog's skin. When you have finished rinsing— and in some cases even before you are through—be ready for the dog to shake the water from its fur. A closed shower curtain can keep the dog from spraying the entire bathroom.

For curly- or longhaired dogs, a coat conditioner is always good as a final step in bathing. The conditioner leaves the coat much more manageable.

Most shorthaired dogs can be towel-dried. This is fun work for kids, and dogs usually love it, too. Medium- and longhaired dogs can be dried partially with a towel and finished with a hair dryer.

Even puppies will need to be bathed, but you must be careful. If the puppy is very young or the weather is cold, use a warm cloth to wet the puppy, rub in a small amount of shampoo, use the cloth to take the soap off, then towel and blow dry.

It is important not to expose your dog to a draft or cool outside temperatures until it is completely dry. Puppies are especially prone to catch a bad cold after a bath even in the spring or summer.

How often you should bathe your dog depends on how much it goes outside, how dirty it gets on a regular basis, and how bad it smells. If you are bathing your dog regularly and it still smells bad, this may indicate a medical problem. To find out the source of the smell, first check the condition of your dog's skin. It might have an infection or a skin allergy. If you find no skin problems, then observe the dog when it is outside to see if it rolls in anything that smells. Many dogs do this after every bath. The third thing to check is its food. It has long been said that a dog smells like what it eats. This is true. A change in your dog's diet might just clear up its odor problem.

94

BATHTIME FOR A
COLLIE FRIEND
OF LASSIE.

A Few Words About Grooming

Many dog breeds, such as poodles, need specific grooming that requires the use of clippers, scissors, knowledge, and skill. There isn't room here to go into the many different grooming techniques and styles for various breeds and looks. If you want to groom your dog yourself, there are books, videos, and classes devoted to the proper grooming of specific breeds. The necessary tools are available at most dog-care outlets. It is wise not to go into this operation without the necessary preparation. Before you try to improve your dog's look through styling and cutting, watch and learn how to do it properly. Once again, a dog show is one of the best places to see the pros in action.

Another grooming myth concerns shaving longhaired dogs in the summer so that they can be cool. In truth, the coats of most longhaired breeds help them stay cool. If you cut the coat, the dog's skin may be exposed to the sun's rays, causing sunburn. Also, the heat that the long hair once helped deflect is now absorbed by the dog, sometimes causing heatstroke. Please consult a vet before shaving a longhaired dog's coat for the summer.

Backyard Detail

Leaving dog mess lying on the ground makes your backyard a very uninviting place. A lidded can with a garbage liner inside can be used to deposit a dog's solid waste every day. Scoopers of various types can be purchased at most stores that handle pet foods or supplies. This simple operation is not only easy to do on a daily basis but takes very little time. The rewards are many. You will have a yard that is usable, children whose feet don't have to be checked before coming inside, fewer flies and other insects that are drawn to the waste products, and a healthier environment for your dog. Another benefit is that you will be able to note your dog's bowel movements. An inconsistent stool is one of the first signs of illness.

After it has been tied properly, the waste can be deposited with your weekly trash for pickup. Some pet supply outlets also stock doggy septic tanks that are easy to install and use.

Include the Kids

Too many times all the work of caring for a dog is left to one person, and usually that person is Mom. Mom has to bathe the dog, brush it, trim its nails, feed and water it, and take it for walks. In order to make sure that the entire family is involved with your dog and has the opportunity to bond with it, assign everyone a task. The best way to do this is have each person volunteer for a specific duty. One person can be in charge of food and water, another the daily walks, another the task of continuing to review obedience commands, and another the grooming and nails. As soon as someone volunteers for the duty, write his or her name on a duty roster and place it where every family member can easily see it. Have a checkoff spot on the roster where each person's job can be marked off each time it is completed. To emphasize the importance of the jobs, tie them to the kids' allowance, television viewing, access to video games, or Internet time. You can also give points for parties and prizes for a job well done. The reward system seems to motivate people of all ages to pull their weight.

The Long-Term Benefits of Daily Care

Of the eight dogs who have been Lassie, only one has died before the age of seventeen. Lassie III died at seven of skin cancer. Most collies rarely see their thirteenth birthday. The reason that the Weatherwaxes' dogs have lived so long has to be their daily interaction with people. Through brushing, yard patrols, hands-on training, and observation, Rudd and Robert Weatherwax have communicated with each Lassie on a daily basis. They knew what was normal and what was unusual for each dog. When a dog was listless, the coat didn't feel or look right, the stools were not consistent, or the eyes watered, the trainers knew immediately and were usually able to treat problems before they developed into something major.

The daily hands-on work also gave each dog a sense of well-being. It is a proven fact that people and animals who are loved and needed get sick less often, recover faster from illness, and live longer.

Daily Care

The secret of these dogs' unusually long lives can be used by you to ensure that your dog will be a vital part of your family for years to come. Just a little time, work, and observation each day will bring mutual benefit to your family and to your dog.

Chapter 8

Basic Obedience Training

*P*eople are drawn to Lassie because of her image, but they are forever *amazed* by what she can do. Lassie would still be beautiful even if she hadn't gone through every level of obedience training and mastered several hundred different commands, but a Lassie who was not well behaved, a Lassie who jumped on people, a Lassie who bolted when she saw a truck and snarled every time she came in contact with another dog would be a dog that amazed no one. Those drawn to Lassie would be repelled if she exhibited negative behavior.

Lassie, the actor, has always lived up to his billing because Robert Weatherwax prepared Lassie to meet the fans' expectations. Almost every dog can do what Lassie does and be the kind of dog Lassie is. The potential is there. The problem is that most people don't invest the time in drawing out those talents.

Basic Obedience Training

Though your dog could probably master two hundred different commands, your family probably doesn't have the time to do the work that would take. Yet for the sake of your family and your dog, there are some basic steps that you both need to complete.

To fully realize the importance of obedience training, your family must understand that dogs love to serve and they love to work. If you have ever seen a guide dog lead a blind person, you have witnessed a dog that is devoted to its owner and its job. Drug-sniffing dogs eagerly search huge mounds of airplane luggage. Lassie is so happy to work on a television-show set that he begs to leave for the set before it is time to go. Lady, my therapy dog, gets excited just getting ready to head for a nursing home to visit with the residents. Yet none of these dogs could do what they do without training. If you want your dog to really be happy and feel fulfilled, even if it is only going to serve your family, then you have to educate your pet.

This chapter focuses on the continuing education of your family's dog. Higher education is vitally important if you want to make your pet a full member of your family. If your dog fails to learn obedience skills, then it will have walls put up that limit its world. When you limit your dog's world, you also deprive your family of many shared experiences.

To function at full potential a person must continue to grow and learn. A child who never learns to read or do math does not have the skills to cope in the real world. A dog that stops with just the three basic commands is limited as well and isn't prepared to travel with you, be mannerly around guests, or act properly around other dogs. A limited education prevents a dog from joining the family in a wide variety of activities.

Your dog cannot train itself but must look to you for guidance. If you and your family make the investment of time and energy in your dog, then all of you benefit. You will also be on the way to having the best dog you have ever known.

Getting Started

Once the basic training—*come, sit,* and *down*—has been completed, many families feel a need to rush into the full range of obedience work. Don't! Like small children, puppies need time to play. As Rudd and Robert Weatherwax have discovered through their years of work, until a dog matures it is better to simply continue to work him through the three basic training commands. A good rule is to wait until a dog is six months old to begin obedience work.

General obedience training can be a family activity. In fact, each member of your family should know how to properly put your dog through its paces, but it is important that everyone does it the same way. If just one person walks on the wrong side of the dog, uses the wrong command, or handles the dog in a manner that is different from the others, the dog will be confused and might unlearn a skill that had taken weeks to grasp. So the golden rule of obedience training is for your family to be consistent. This means that everyone, dog and family, is being trained at the same time. This approach makes training a real learning experience, creates respect and admiration for your dog, and builds a bond that will last forever. Using the Lassie method, I have seen four-year-old children perfectly control a big dog! At the age of eight, my son took our Lady and beat out more than forty other dogs in an area dog obedience and trick competition.

Teaching a dog obedience training is not hard, but it does take time. But even if it means waiting an extra month, make sure you and your family have the spare hours to devote to this education. To do this job right, at least one member of your family must devote at least thirty minutes each day to the work. This educational process will last several months, and as with a child's schooling, it is vitally important that you do not cheat, skip days, or fail to do homework. Once you begin, you must stay the course, or your time will count for nothing.

By now you may be thinking, "Wouldn't it be better to turn this obedience training over to a professional?" It is tempting, yet there are several reasons to do the work yourself.

There are many excellent obedience schools, and many use very loving techniques to train dogs. But a bond will be missing if you and your family are not involved in the training process. An educated dog will come back from school and figure out that you and your family don't know what you are doing. If you are not able to speak the same language as your dog, and your dog doesn't respect your authority, then you will have wasted your money and your dog's time. If your dog goes to school, then find a way for a family member to go with the animal.

If you want to seek outside guidance in obedience work, then the best source might just be a local dog club that provides weekly lessons for dogs and their owners. In this kind of class a member of your family and your dog will be trained as one, learning obedience at the same time in the same way. Even if you choose this route, daily training sessions will still be required, and the family member who is taking the classes must be responsible for properly training the other members of the family to handle the dog. In other words, there are shortcuts, but they still require work and time. To best establish the family bond, everyone needs to get involved.

The Classroom

Choose a place to train your dog that you can use for every training session. The backyard, a park, a schoolyard, or even a vacant lot is fine, but you must be able to use this same classroom setting each day so that your dog can concentrate on you and not the changing scene.

Training sessions should be done at least two but not more than three times a day. These sessions should last at least ten minutes, but no longer than thirty. Like most children, a dog becomes bored and distracted when training lasts too long.

You need to make a commitment to training every day. Sometimes illness or weather might prevent a session, but try to work around both. When you miss a day, it takes several days of review to get back to where you were before the training was interrupted. So have a backup plan. A family member can step in as a substitute teacher as long as the training is done the same way and with the same commands.

Most obedience courses begin with the three basic commands—*come, sit,* and *down.* Your dog should already know these three very well. If not, review them now. Make sure your pet can do all three automatically.

Heel

102

Heel means to stay at the side of the master, never wandering ahead or lagging behind. Every dog should learn this task.

With the collar and chain fitted properly on the dog, stand on your dog's right. Your left hand will be closest to your dog.

UNTIL YOUR DOG
LEARNS HOW TO
HEEL PROPERLY,
WALKING HIM
WILL NOT BE
VERY MUCH FUN
FOR YOU OR
THE DOG.

Keeping the end loop of the leash in your right hand, hold the remainder of the leash in your left hand, about a foot above the dog's shoulder. This will vary depending on the size of the dog. Any extra leash can be folded or looped and held in the right hand. Your left hand should hold the leash firmly enough above the dog's shoulders to keep the dog in straight, standing posture. Now ask your dog to heel, then move forward, stepping first with the left leg because it is closest to the dog. Your pet will soon learn to start when you do. Keep the leash short in order to keep the dog beside your leg. Don't allow it to wander or control the pace. Stay in charge.

At first you may be tugging the leash to slow the dog down or speed it up. This is to be expected. Urge the dog on with positive prodding when it is a step ahead or behind. When the dog is beside you, walking at your pace, give praise. When you have walked ten or twelve yards, stop and ask your dog to sit, then give a treat and lavish a great deal more praise.

At first some dogs feel nervous walking right beside someone in the *heel* position. An old Weatherwax teaching trick for the *heel* command is to place a fence or wall on the dog's left. With the wall on one side and the master on the other, the dog has to walk right beside you and cannot edge away to the left.

The key things to remember when working with the heel command:

Keep the dog on your left (the dog's right).
Keep the dog beside you so that your left hand is over its shoulders.
Always say *heel* before you start. If you develop a hand signal for this command, use that as well.
Always finish with a great deal of praise.

103

Stay

Teaching the *stay* command can be trying for both your family and the dog. Yet this simple command is so very important. A dog that knows *stay* can be trusted anywhere.

Several years ago I spoke at a banquet in Wisconsin. Robert Weatherwax and Lassie were there with me. During the dinner, Robert took Lassie off the leash, asked him to lie down, then asked him to stay. Among hundreds of people eating prime rib with all the trimmings, flash cameras taking pictures, and people talking and pointing, Lassie remained in his spot for more than an hour. He was happy to do what Robert had asked. Lassie's ability to stay not only kept him from begging for food from hundreds of people but allowed Robert to enjoy dinner without worrying about Lassie's wandering off. Imagine if you could trust your dog this much!

There are a number of different variations of the *stay* command. At the banquet in Wisconsin, Robert used a *long stay* command with Lassie in the down position. Training should begin with the *sit stay*.

You will need at least a twenty-foot lead. If your leash is not long enough, tie a cord onto the loop. Ask your dog to sit, then slowly walk a few feet away. As you leave, ask your dog to stay. Of course the dog will try to follow you. When it makes a move, stop the dog, and ask it to sit again. After the dog has sat for a few seconds, ask it to stay, and then move away again.

At first the dog may stay in the sitting position for only a few seconds. That is fine. Reward the dog with a treat and praise for its efforts. Then begin again. Over time the dog will learn what *stay* means, and you will be able to move a great distance while the dog continues to hold its position. For the first few days always return to the dog before allowing it to get up. After a few days, when you are sure the dog knows what you want, call the dog to you when it has held its position for an appropriate amount of time. Always reward your dog with praise and treats.

The *down stay* is just like the *sit stay* except that you place your dog in the down position first. If your dog has *sit stay* figured out, then *down stay* will be easy.

Remember, once your dog has been told to stay, it must stay. This means you should be able to walk away and hide, step over the dog, even have a football game all around it, and it should stay until released from the command. To work on the *long stay,* ask your dog to stay for longer and longer periods of time (up to five minutes). Hide from the dog but keep an eye on it. If it moves, scold it gently, then ask it to stay again. Always reward your dog for its work!

105

STAY IS A FUNDAMENTALLY IMPORTANT COMMAND THAT EVERY DOG SHOULD KNOW. THIS IS THE SIT STAY.

An old Weatherwax trick is to give the *stay* command while holding your hand about a foot in front of your dog's eyes. Even Rudd couldn't have told you why this hand command always helps in the exercise, but it does. Dogs seem to naturally associate a hand in front of the face with *stay*.

Stand

Sometimes dogs in the stay or down position don't always get up when asked. The best way to get your dog to get up is to stand to its right, then ask it to stand while you gently place your foot under its stomach. Don't kick, don't prod, don't do anything that would hurt the dog, but gently lift your foot just a little. Your dog will get up.

Stand is a command that most dogs don't have any problem with. When they are on the lead and excited about being with you, they want to stand and go!

Off Leash

A dog that has been properly trained in obedience work will perform just as well off a leash as on. If your dog can now perfectly perform *come, sit, down, heel,* and *stay* with every member of your family, you can attempt this next step in the training process.

Your dog should know what to do, but without the leash it might want to challenge your control. In this case you must take charge with an assertive nature and voice. Continue to ask the dog to work with you, but let it know who is in charge. If the dog simply will not respond to you without the leash, scold the dog and then replace the lead. Spend a few more days working with the leash attached. After the dog has proven itself again, try off-lead work again.

When you are working with the obedience training off-lead,

106

HEELING
WITHOUT A
LEASH SIGNALS
THAT A DOG
IS VERY WELL
TRAINED.

make sure you are in a safe area. You don't want your dog to be injured or to injure another animal or person. If you are in a park or an open area, look around. If traffic is too close, if large groups of people are involved in a number of distracting activities, or if others are working their animals, find somewhere else to train or temporarily go back to working with the leash.

If while working without a leash your dog bolts away, call the dog back but don't run after it. If you run, your dog will see it as a game and run away from you. Walk up to the dog, saying its name gently. If your dog is more interested in playing than in following your commands, put it back on the lead and save this training for a few weeks or months, until the dog is more mature. It is important to remember that, like children, dogs do not mature at the same rate. Even littermates vary in the age at which they can learn.

107

Off-lead work is important because it gives your family control of your dog in every situation. If the dog respects the family members, knows the rules, and receives praise for doing things properly, then it will be a dog you can take anywhere.

Several years ago I watched a dog rush after a squirrel in a city park. The squirrel raced across a road, and the dog started to follow it. At that very moment there was a truck coming down the road at a high rate of speed. There was no doubt in my mind that the dog was doomed. Then from across the park a boy about ten years old yelled out, "Rex! *Stay!*" The dog immediately quit running and stopped a few feet from the road. Rex's life was saved because he had been through obedience work, and he and his master had learned their lessons well.

Go

One of the activities in the *Lassie* television show that sometimes gets made fun of is Lassie going to get help. Everyone remembers at least one of the scenes in which Timmy or Jeff would get in trouble and tell Lassie, "Go get Mom, girl."

Lassie would immediately race off and bring help. You may have laughed at this plot device, but your dog can learn to do this, too.

Going to a place or a person is one of the easiest things to teach a dog. First, put the dog on a leash. If you want the dog to go to its bed, say, "Samson, go to your bed." Then lead him to his bed and ask him to stay. Reward him and repeat the exercise. In just a few days Samson will know what you mean when you ask him to go to his bed.

You can expand your dog's vocabulary to include several different places. As you can imagine, this command is wonderful when your dog is bothering guests or getting in the way of work that is being done around the house—which leads to the point of not abusing that power. Use this command only when necessary, and always reward your dog for doing what it is asked.

Your dog can also be taught to go to a particular person. Once again using the lead, ask your dog to take you to a member of your family, then lead your dog to him or her. Don't forget to reward your dog. In a matter of only a few days, your dog will know every member of your family by name and will be able to bring them to you.

A Final Word About Obedience

Obedience trials are open to any breed of dog, including mutts. A dog that has learned all the things necessary to win an obedience championship will not only be a dog with a trophy but a dog whose family has a valuable best friend. It goes without saying that a well-trained dog will amaze your friends, be more involved in your family's life, and steal your heart.

Chapter 9

Tricks of the Trade

As Robert Weatherwax will tell you, Lassie is an actor. He doesn't perform tricks or stunts as much as he takes direction and "sells" his part in front of a camera. Real trick dogs perform in carnivals and on television variety shows. While the script may call for Lassie to do different things each day, most trick dogs learn and repeat the same routine every time they perform. Yet even though Lassie must respond to a different set of instructions almost every time he works—which is far more complicated than repeating a learned show many years in a row—special tricks are a part of Lassie's life, too. To be the actor he is, Lassie must learn hundreds of special tricks, remember them, and perform them perfectly when asked.

Most of the nine dogs who have played Lassie have been able to respond to at least two hundred different commands. A few have learned more than three hundred. How many your dog can learn depends a great deal on its native intelligence, the time spent in training, and its teacher. If you have the time and your dog has the ability, the sky really is the limit.

Most people understand why it is so important for Robert Weatherwax to teach Lassie hundreds of different stunts and tricks, but many wonder why a family dog should learn them. After all, your dog is probably not going to have its own television show or go on the road with a circus. What good will it do your dog?

While it seems that almost everyone marvels at a dog that does things beyond basic obedience commands, most don't realize that stopping training with just obedience work is like allowing your children to leave school after eighth grade. The more a dog learns, the more chances it has to enlarge its and your family's world.

When your family is with your dog in a public place, after "What's his name?" and "What breed is he?" the question you are probably most often asked is "Does he know any tricks?" Wouldn't it be great if you could not only say yes but allow your dog to show its stuff? I guarantee that as much as you will enjoy showing off your dog to others, your dog will enjoy it more.

What You Need to Get Started

The tools for this part of your dog's education are much the same as for basic training and obedience work. You will need your slip-chain collar and leash, your treats, patience, a place with few distractions where you can work, and about a half hour each day. You will also want your doggy dictionary so that you and your children can record the various commands and hand signals for each stunt. After a while you will probably have so many pages filled that even you will be amazed by your dog's vocabulary.

111

Even if your dog is very intelligent and learns quickly, don't go too fast. Set a goal for your dog to learn one trick a week. Then add new ones after your dog has passed several examinations. Even if it seems to know them as well as it knows its name, don't forget to continue to review the old tricks each day, too. This review should include all the obedience training your dog has had so far.

Unlike obedience work, learning tricks or stunts does not build from a foundation. What this means is that if your dog cannot grasp a trick after you have tried to teach it for several days, move on to another. A few tricks are interconnected, but most are independent of one another. So if your dog can't seem to learn to fetch, don't worry about it. While retrievers almost always love bringing things back to you, many herding dogs just don't like the idea of continually going after the same object. It is not a part of their nature. So find the tricks best suited to your dog, and center on those.

With all of these stunts, don't allow the dog to do something until you ask it to. Some dogs will want a treat so badly that they will perform before getting the commands, trying to guess what you want them to do. Make sure everyone in the family knows not to reward your dog for guessing.

Even though I am not emphasizing hand signals in this chapter, the hand or silent commands for each trick will usually be obvious to you. Your body language will give you away. If you do use silent commands, describe or draw them in your doggy dictionary.

Left and Right

At first glance, teaching a dog the difference between its left and right might seem complicated. In reality, this is one of the easiest exercises to teach any dog.

Your dog will need to be on a leash. Stand in front of it and make sure it is facing you. If you have a large dog, this trick can best be taught by someone who is fairly tall. If your dog is small, a child can easily teach left from right.

112

CIRCLING LEFT AND RIGHT IS A WONDERFUL STUNT FOR ANY DOG WHO LIKES TO PERFORM. BEST OF ALL, IT IS EASY TO TEACH.

When you have your dog's attention, ask it to go right. You can say, "Go right, Boy, I want you to go right." Be sure to emphasize the word *right*. Hold a treat in your free hand above the dog's head, place the leash above its head, and lead the dog to the right (your left). Continue to lead the dog in a clockwise circle until it has returned to its starting point. Then reward and praise the dog.

Working with the treat, continue to lead your dog in a circle several more times, and you will notice two things happening. Your dog will begin to turn tighter and tighter circles, and it will also go faster and faster. Keep working the dog with the lead for several days. After it knows how to turn a right circle without your leading it with the leash, begin asking your dog to go right when the lead is not attached. At first you may have to continue leading the dog with a treat. When the dog fully understands *right,* teach it *left* in the same way.

Once the dog has both *left* and *right* down independently, you can begin to mix them together. If the dog confuses one with the other, ask the dog to do it again and show the way to go. Soon the dog will get the directions right every time.

For a hand signal, raise your right hand and spin it in the direction you want your dog to turn. It will come to understand this as well as it does the words *right* and *left*.

Shake Hands

Shake hands is one of the most basic dog tricks. It is also something that many people will ask your dog to do. You begin the exercise by putting your dog in front of you in the sitting

ONE OF THE FIRST THINGS PEOPLE OFTEN ASK IS, "CAN YOUR DOG SHAKE?" IN THIS CASE, YOUR DOG CAN ANSWER FOR YOU.

113

position. Ask the dog to shake by saying, "Shake hands, Boy, shake!" Then reach out with your left hand and tap the back side of its right paw until the dog lifts it to meet your extended right hand. Shake the paw gently, being careful not to squeeze too tight. As you hold its paw, give the dog a treat with your left hand and praise the dog.

Teaching a dog to shake hands is usually very easy. A dog quickly grasps what will earn it praise and a treat. The key thing for children and adults to remember is to make sure you have asked your dog to sit first. While you can teach your dog to shake with either paw, it is best that it learn to use its right paw in order not to confuse those who want to shake with the dog.

Right and Left Paw

114

You can take the first two tricks and combine them to teach your dog a simple trick that many people find quite impressive.

Begin with your dog sitting down. Have a table or chair in front of the dog that is low enough for it to easily set its paw on. Then say, "Right paw, Boy, give me your right paw." After your command, lift its paw up and place it on the table. Hold it there for a few seconds, then reward the dog with a treat and praise. Continue to work with the right paw until the dog knows the command. Then add *left paw*. A fun addition to this command is using the term *southpaw* in your command. When you ask the dog for its left foot, say, "Southpaw, Boy, give me your southpaw."

In your dictionary be sure to note that with this command you start with *right paw*, while on the command to go to the right you begin with *go right*. If you begin both commands with the word *right*, you will confuse your dog.

Speak

Speak is a command that mystifies most people. They can't seem to understand how to get a dog to bark when they want him to. The first step is to get your dog excited by playing with it in a very energetic manner. When a dog is trying to grab a ball or toy out of your hand, it will almost always bark. While you are playing, say *speak* over and over again until the dog barks, then praise it and reward it for doing so.

Rudd Weatherwax used to teach dogs to speak in another way. He would tie a dog to a post or tree, then offer a special treat that was just out of reach. As he did, he would ask the dog to speak. The anxious dog always would, and by doing so would earn a reward. Soon the dog associated the word *speak* with a reward and would be trained.

BEING ABLE TO SPEAK ON COMMAND MAY NOT BE VERY IMPORTANT TO A DOG OR A FAMILY'S LIFE, BUT IT IS ALWAYS AN IMPRESSIVE TRICK.

115

Fetch

The key to this trick is to find something your dog really likes. Most dogs have favorite toys; some like balls, others Frisbees. Most dogs are also very protective of their toys. They don't like to share them. When your dog has bonded with a toy, let the dog play with it for a while, then suddenly take it and roll it a few feet away. The dog will naturally go to get it. As it does, say, "Fetch it, Boy, fetch it." When the dog grabs the toy, praise it and give it a treat. Then try the trick again, throwing the toy a little farther this time.

Many dogs don't like to bring the item back at first. They will either run away with it or just play with it where they pick it up. To make sure your dog completes the exercise, don't reward it with a treat until it has dropped the object at your feet or in your hand. You can usually accomplish this by simply calling the dog to you and then offering the treat. Even a favorite toy rarely compares to a chunk of jerky, so your dog will drop the toy to eat.

Once the dog associates rewards with fetching, it will want to play all the time. The dog can also learn to fetch just about anything. Like playing pitch and catch with your son or daughter, there is something about fetch that is a great deal of fun for parents and children. Most dogs love it, too.

For dogs who love to swim, a variation of this trick can be used at a pond or lake. Make sure the area is not dangerous for your family or your dog, and make sure that the item to be retrieved will float. Toss an object out in the water and ask your dog to fetch it. Don't try this with a dog that doesn't like water, or you will have to fetch it yourself.

Get the Paper

Begin this learning exercise by taking your dog with you to retrieve the morning paper. Say to your dog, "Get the paper, Boy, get me the paper." The key word is *paper*. Once you have asked the dog to bring the paper to you, pick the paper up and put it in the dog's mouth. Then walk the dog back to the house. If the dog drops the paper, once again ask the dog to pick it up; place it in the dog's mouth if necessary. When you get inside the house, take the paper from the dog, give the earned treat, and praise the dog.

If you want your dog to learn this exercise quickly, have several old papers wrapped and make a few trips to where your paper is usually dropped. If the dog knows *fetch*, it will probably learn this quickly.

Two areas of special caution: Be careful of traffic, and go at least partway with your dog while watching the road so that your dog doesn't get hit by a car. If your dog is not disciplined enough to go straight out, get the paper, and then come back to the house—if your dog tends to wander—then keep a very watchful eye. Make sure the dog doesn't forget the job and dash off to explore the neighborhood.

Some dogs really enjoy fetching things. Be careful that your dog knows to bring only your paper to your door, or your neighbors might find their morning edition missing!

FETCH IS NOT JUST A TRICK—IT'S A GAME MOST DOGS LOVE!

Catch

Some dogs are like Babe Ruth or Ken Griffey, Jr. They just naturally love to play ball. Getting them to fetch or catch is easy. Yet for most dogs it takes a while to understand how to catch an object. Make sure the object you are throwing to your dog is very soft, such as a tennis ball. If it is hard, it could break the dog's teeth.

Ask your dog to sit, then move a couple of feet away from it. Get it excited by waving the ball up and down and back and forth. The dog's attention should be focused on your hand and the ball. Then toss the ball in a gentle arc while saying, "Catch it, Boy, catch it." If the dog lets the ball fall to the ground before picking it up, gently scold the dog. Get the ball and try again from closer range. In some cases you will have to start by dropping the ball from just a few inches above your dog's nose. When your dog finally catches the ball, praise it, take the ball away, and immediately give him a treat. As your dog gets better at catching, move a bit farther away. Even if your dog is very good, don't move back too far. Too long a toss might hurt the dog. Find its maximum safe range and stick with it.

Some trainers teach *catch* by having their dogs first catch a treat. While this will usually work if you have food, your dog will never want to catch anything that isn't edible. Thus it becomes a very limited trick.

Yes and No

This is an easy trick for a dog to learn. If you have seen the very early episodes of *Lassie*, you probably saw the character of Jeff teach this one as a part of the show. Have your dog sit in front of you. Hold a treat in your hands and get the dog's attention. As it stares in anticipation of the treat, move your hand from side to side so that the dog's head moves to follow you. As you do, say, "Is the answer *no*?" Then give the dog a treat. In just a few days the dog will be able to answer any question you ask by shaking its head when it hears the key word *no*.

Yes is taught the same way except that you move the treat up and down to get the dog to nod. As you do this, say, "Is the answer *yes*?"

If you plan to perform using the *yes* and *no* responses, you might want to teach different key words or have your dog learn this trick with signals. Then the dog could answer any question correctly just by hearing a certain expression, such as "What do you think, Boy?" for *yes* or "How do you feel about that?" for *no*. Hand commands make this even easier for your dog. Then all it has to do is wait for your signal to give its reply.

Kiss

This is a trick that many mothers hate. Moms just don't seem to like a dog's licking their kids' faces. In truth, it shouldn't pose a danger to the child or the dog.

Teaching a dog to kiss is very simple. If you lean down next to its face, your dog will probably lick you on the cheek. It is a natural reaction. As it does, say, "Kiss me. Give me a kiss." Reward the dog after it has given you a lick.

If the dog doesn't naturally lick your face, then use a drop of honey to sweeten the target. Put the honey on your cheek,

A LITTLE
HONEY ON
THE CHEEK
SHOULD GET
YOU A KISS.

ask to be kissed, and place your cheek by the dog's nose. When it licks the honey, praise and reward the dog.

Yawn

Although it might stun some people, teaching a dog to yawn on cue is one of the hardest tricks you and your dog can try to master. First you have to wait for your dog to yawn, observe the dog as it does so, quickly say, "Yawn, Boy, yawn," then praise and reward the dog. In order for the dog to understand what you want, you have to catch it yawning several more times over the course of many days.

Are there any shortcuts? You can try to pry open your dog's mouth as you say, "Yawn." To do this you need to place one hand under the back part of its jaw so that your fingertips reach up to the sides of its mouth. A bit of slight pressure will cause your dog to open its mouth. Through repetition your dog will learn to drop its jaw on its own. Still, its yawn will appear far more realistic and impressive if you can teach it by having it imitate a real yawn.

Sit Up and Beg

Many people are very impressed with any dog who can sit up and look as though it is begging. In truth, this is really not much of a trick. Small, light dogs can master it in no time if you simply hold a treat just out of reach above them. But for larger dogs, sitting up is not that easy and very unnatural. Once you teach them how to balance, then even most large dogs lose their fear of this trick.

If you want to teach your dog to sit up, start by having it sit in the corner of a room as you kneel in front of it. Place the leash on the dog, then say, "Beg, Boy. Come on, beg." The reason you should avoid saying "sit up" is that your dog may react to the first word only and stay in a seated position. After you ask the dog to beg, pull up easily on the leash, then lift its front paws with your free hand until they are almost under the dog's chin. The walls against its back and sides should help the dog feel secure so that it won't be worried about losing its balance and falling.

It may take you a while to get your dog to go up on its own. If your dog is older, it might just not want to do this trick. If it does master it in the corner, tell the dog to beg in the middle of the room. When the dog does it right, remember to reward and praise it.

Crawl

This command was probably first used in training army dogs to pass easily under a barbed-wire fence. When Lassie played a service dog in his second movie, *Son of Lassie*, Rudd Weatherwax developed the following method for teaching dogs to crawl.

Have your dog on a leash and ask it to go to the down position. Stand at an angle in front and slightly to your dog's right side, holding the leash in your left hand. As you say, "Crawl, Boy, crawl," begin to urge or lightly pull the dog forward. Do not let it get up. If it starts to get on its feet, say, "Down," continue to pull, and again ask the dog to crawl.

For your dog's sake, do this exercise on ground that does not have rough growth or rocks that could hurt it. Find someplace that is crawl-friendly. The best way to know how your dog will feel as it crawls is to get on your knees and crawl over the same area. If it hurts you, it will hurt your dog, too.

On Your Side

This is not a natural position for dogs because it reveals their throat and belly for easy attack. Instinct tells every dog that this is not wise. So have patience when teaching this trick.

Put your dog in a down position, then say, "Side, Boy. Get on your side." Standing or kneeling beside the dog's right side, pull on the leash with your right hand and push the dog's shoulder with your left hand. This action will pull the dog's head down and roll its body over. Help the dog hold the position for a few moments, then praise and reward it. Continue to repeat the training in this fashion until you can feel that the dog is going down before you pull the leash or push with your hand.

After the dog has completely mastered *on your side* from a down position, begin to do it from a standing position. First ask the dog to go down, then, after it has held that position for a full count (about a second), ask it to get on its side.

Roll Over

If you have a big dog or a dog with a long back, such as a basset hound, you should pass on this trick. Rolling over can be very hard on a long or a large dog's spine. The twisting can cause real damage.

If you have a dog like a Jack Russell terrier, this trick can be a great deal of fun for both of you. Frank Inn, who worked with Rudd Weatherwax and Lassie for years and then moved on to work with his own dog, Benji, always used *roll over* to charm his audiences.

Begin with the *on your side* command, then bend over

beside your dog, place your foot on the leash, leaving it slightly slack, and put your right hand on your dog's nearest shoulder while you pick up its front two paws in your left hand. As you say, "Roll over, Boy. Let's roll over," push the shoulder as you lift the two paws and roll the dog over. This will probably frighten the dog at first, so it will take a while for the dog to do it on its own. When the dog gets the hang of it and realizes how amazed people are by this trick, it will roll one way and then the other just to impress its audience.

Open Door

Teaching a dog to open a door can be a mistake. Robert Weatherwax once left home to go to the store, and while he was gone, Lassie VII opened the back door, went into the yard, opened the gate, strolled down the block, let a few neighborhood dogs out of their yards, and brought them all back home with him. They were all waiting in the living room when Robert returned.

Lassie VII also learned how to open the refrigerator, and you can imagine the trouble it caused. Until Robert obtained a Lassie-proof lock, midnight snacks were the rule of the house.

The easy way to teach your dog how to open a door is to cover a knob with a tennis ball. You can accomplish this by carefully cutting the side of the ball just enough to slip it over the knob. Next, adjust the door so that it can be opened with only a slight turn. With the leash on and your dog standing in front of the closed door, say, "Open the door, Boy, open the door," then pull its muzzle up to the tennis ball. Help the dog grab the ball. This can be accomplished much more easily if the dog has been playing fetch with the same ball over the past few weeks. When the dog grabs the ball, use your hand to make the dog hold it, then gently push its head downward. The turning motion should easily open the door. This is one trick that some dogs just can't learn, and it was one of the hardest ones for Lassie. If your dog doesn't want to do it, don't push it. Besides, if your dog doesn't learn this trick, you don't have to worry about its leaving without you.

Pick Up and Carry

Begin this lesson by picking up a ball or stick and placing it in your dog's mouth. If the dog has already learned to fetch, this should be easy. As you place the object in its mouth, say, "Carry it, Boy, carry it." Walk with the dog heeling and carrying the object for a few steps, even if you have to help the dog hold the object in its mouth. Then stop and praise your dog.

When your dog has learned to carry several different objects, drop one of them on the ground in front of the dog and ask it to pick up the object. Snap your fingers and point to the object to show the dog where it is. If necessary, push the dog's head down and place the object in its mouth as you repeat the command.

When the dog learns to pick up the object, have it learn *drop it*. The first time, just take the object from its mouth. After several more tries, drop your hand a little below its mouth and repeat the command. Soon you can ask the dog to drop it, and the dog will respond by letting it fall out of its mouth.

If you can use three or four distinctively different objects, you can make this trick more impressive by teaching your dog which is a ball, a stick, a toy, or a piece of rope. In order for your dog to learn the difference, you must always identify each object when you teach this stunt. After several weeks of working with each object separately and in different training sessions, and after many reminders from you as what each object is called, set out two objects and ask your dog to pick up just one of them. After your dog learns to sort these two, add a third and then a fourth.

Bring by the Hand

You can teach your dog to take someone by the hand with its mouth and lead the person to you. This trick never fails to impress people and is a lesson that will take two members of your family. It combines *pick it up, come,* and *drop it.* Your dog's cue will be your saying, "Bring her to me, Boy, bring her to me."

Have your dog stand beside your helper. When you ask the dog to *bring her to me,* push the dog's head to your helper's hand and say, "Pick it up." If the dog doesn't understand what is to be picked up, open its jaws and place your helper's hand in them. If necessary—and it usually is—have your helper hold her hand in your dog's mouth as you move away a few feet and call the dog to you. If the dog is confused, have your helper lead the dog to you while keeping her hand in its mouth.

Usually the dog will want to drop your helper's hand, then walk to you. If it does, start again. Say to the dog, "Bring her to me," have your dog *pick it up*—again showing the dog your helper's hand. Walk away and call the dog again. When the dog finally leads your helper to you, thank the dog and tell it to "drop it." The dog should let go of the hand.

After your dog can do this well with one person, add to this trick. Because you taught your dog the *go to* command in your obedience work, you can now make this *bring her to me* command really impressive. All you have to do is get your dog to bring a certain person. Begin by having the dog bring a member of the family he knows, who is in sight and only a few feet away from you. When the dog can do this, ask the dog to pick out a person it knows from several others and bring him or her to you. "Go to Jane, Boy. Bring Jane to me." Finally, when the dog does this very well, have it go to get someone who is in another room.

125

After your dog has learned this trick, Timmy telling Lassie to go get Mom won't seem nearly as unbelievable.

Pray

Like most advanced tricks, teaching your dog to pray simply combines or modifies tricks it has already learned. First you must teach your dog to put both paws on a table, chair, or bed. This is like the *right paw* and *southpaw* commands combined. The command that will help you break this down is *both paws*.

When your dog has learned to put its right paw on a table, chair, or bed, tell it to put "both paws." Tap under the dog's left paw, lifting if necessary, until it has placed the paw beside the right one. Work on *both paws* until the dog does it without having to go to the right paw first.

When your dog has learned *both paws*, tell the dog, "Say your prayers." When you speak to the dog, push its head down to meet its paws and hold it there. As always, praise and reward you dog as it learns each step. This is the most important facet of dog training.

Bow

At the end of a show a good performer always bows. To begin this training lesson, make your dog *stand* and *stay*. Then, while standing on the dog's right, use your right hand to push your dog's front legs forward. Keep your left hand under the back of your dog's belly so that it won't lie down. As you are doing this, say, "Bow, Boy, bow for your fans." When its front legs are down and its elbows are touching the ground, gently push its head down so that it rests on top of its paws. Hold it for a moment, then let the dog return to a standing position. Praise and reward the dog, and repeat the exercise.

If your dog cannot seem to bow without your holding up its back end, you can place a two-by-four on the ground just in front of its back legs. When the dog begins to lie down, it will

A BOW IS THE BEST WAY
TO END ANY
PERFORMANCE.

127

feel the board and naturally raise its hindquarters. Within a few lessons the dog shouldn't need any help at all.

Bowing is a great deal like a dog's natural stretching, so this trick really just asks your dog to do something it already does several times a day. Still, be patient. It may take the dog a while to link bowing to anything else.

A Second Look

While the tricks and commands you have learned here represent only a small portion of the ones Lassie knows, you probably now have a real understanding of how Rudd and Robert Weatherwax trained Lassie to meet all those unique acting challenges in movies and on television. With this foundation, you can probably fit more and more of these lessons together so that you, your family, and your dog can put on a very special show that will charm everyone who gets the opportunity to see your dog work. Best of all, when your family members understand how to break down training lessons into steps and then build on these steps, they can invent their own original stunts.

This is a great educational opportunity for everyone. Essentially, this is what Robert does for Lassie each time he finds something new in a script.

When your family is working on new tricks for your dog, remember to add the commands to your doggy dictionary. And make sure that whatever you are teaching your dog is safe and won't get him into trouble. Teaching a dog to dig is not that important, and once rewarded for it, the dog might just dig a swimming pool–size hole for you. So think before you teach.

Chapter 10

Problems and Solutions

No dog is perfect—not even Lassie. Every dog has behavioral problems that must be addressed. Many of these problems arise because of a simple lack of supervision, some are unique to a breed, some touch every dog at one time or another, and some are just the result of a lack of training. Can every bad habit be fixed? No! But most can be, and the few that remain can be dealt with in a positive fashion.

Pal, the first Lassie, was one of the best-mannered dogs that ever worked in the movies or lived with a family. Yet even this magnificent collie had one bad habit that Rudd Weatherwax couldn't break. Like most people, Pal didn't like the noise of motorcycles. When one drove by, he barked from the moment he heard it until it was completely out of sight. While he didn't mind cars or trucks, for some reason he viewed a motorcycle as a monster. Why? Rudd never knew, but he guessed that Pal must have been frightened or traumatized by a motorcycle before he came to the Weatherwax home. Though the trainer continued to address the problem throughout Pal's life, in this one area he never gained full control. Pal continued to bark at every motorcycle he saw.

This chapter highlights and discusses methods of stopping disruptive or destructive behavior. The tactics presented have been tested by many dog trainers and owners, and they work in almost all cases. Give each solution a fair shake. It might take a bit of patience and a lot of time, but in most cases you will be able to deal with your dog's problems.

Jumping on People

Jumping up on people is one of the most common acts of an ill-mannered dog. The reasons for this behavior are largely innate. Dogs often greet each other this way, and they are usually excited around people and want to get their attention. If you have a large dog, then the problem of jumping must be addressed for safety reasons. A German shepherd can knock a full-grown adult down, so imagine what this dog could do to a small child or a fragile senior citizen. From the standpoint of safety alone, you have to stop a dog's jump-greeting.

One of the best ways to stop this behavior is not to allow it to start. If you have a puppy, don't pick it up by its front legs when you greet it, and don't allow it to jump on you. If it does, you can stop this behavior by saying no and then holding on to its front paws and squeezing tightly until the pup decides it doesn't like it. Continue to do this every time the pup jumps on you. The key to making your dog understand not to use the jump-greeting is making sure that no one in your family continues to encourage its jumping. If family members are not consistent, you will fight a never-ending battle.

Small adult dogs can be handled much like puppies. Saying

a firm no and squeezing the front paws will usually work over time. In larger dogs, using your knee to push (not kick or thrust) against the dog's rib cage will cause the dog to go down on all fours. It is important not to kick the dog or apply anything more than light pressure with your knee. You do not want to hurt or injure your dog, just teach it to stay on the ground.

If your dog knows the obedience commands, you can usually stop it with a *sit* command before it jumps. The importance of obedience work with every dog cannot be stressed too much. It can help you with every facet of your dog's life.

If your dog is a habitual jumper, it will take time to effect a change in its greeting behavior. Yet if your family is in agreement and no one is working against the goal, this bad habit can be stopped.

Barking Inside

Many dogs want to bark or howl when left alone in a house. If you live in the country, this is not a problem, but if you have neighbors close by, the howling dog syndrome can cause you and your neighbors a lot of grief.

Before you can fix the problem, you need to try to find out what is causing it. Dogs bark and howl for many reasons. Some do it to voice their loneliness, others don't like the quiet, some are bored, some need or want to go outside, and others just seem to like to hear themselves.

If you believe your dog is lonely or doesn't like a home without noise, then try leaving a radio or television on while you are gone. A great many times the simple act of having human voices playing from a box will solve the problem.

If you determine that your dog is bored, try leaving something for it to do. A chew toy might entertain the dog. Some trainers put peanut butter inside a toy and leave it for the dog. Even if the dog can't reach the peanut butter, it will continue to try for hours. Then, when it is worn out, it will probably sleep.

If activities and noise don't work, then you will have to go to some effort to break the bad habit.

Make sure your dog thinks you are leaving it alone. Put it in a room by itself and close the door. Don't make any noise. If you can, go outside and wait beside an open window. When the dog begins to bark, use your disembodied voice to say "No! Quiet!" This will confuse the dog. You are not there, it can't see you, but you are still asking it to stop what it is doing. In most cases, after a few minutes, it will begin barking again. When it does, again say, "No! Quiet!" Don't use the dog's name, just continue calling out your simple orders as needed. Be prepared for the long haul—bring a book and a chair and continue your work until your dog has stopped barking for at least two hours. When this much time has passed between barks, you have probably made your point and begun to win your battle. Still, you may have to repeat the trial several more times over the next few weeks before you can be sure the problem has been solved.

Barking Outside

A dog that barks outside in the yard may be trying to tell you something. The dog might want you to know that it is bored and wants to come in. It may be answering the bark of another dog down the street. It might be seeing something that it wants everyone else to see, too. It might be barking just because it thinks its voice is wonderful.

The two most successful ways to address barking are with noise and water. Dogs don't seem to like either. If your dog is barking excessively and disturbing the whole neighborhood, get ready for action.

Initially you might want to tie a few tin cans together, put them in a place where you can pick them up quickly, and wait for your dog to go into action. Every time it barks more than just a couple of times, open the door and toss the cans out. The noise will cause the dog to stop, and it won't like the sound at all.

Repeating this a few times might just cure your dog of the problem. If not, go to plan B.

Dogs don't like to be sprayed with water. Most toy stores and discount outlets carry large, very powerful water guns. These new types of guns usually don't leak, carry huge amounts of water, are battery powered, and can shoot as far as fifty feet. To prepare for battle, hide and then wait for your dog to start barking. When it does, shoot the dog with a stream of water. It won't take long for your dog to associate the water with the barking. In most cases the dog will quit and bark only when it is trying to warn you of real danger.

A final method of trying to stop excessive barking is by catching the dog in the act, holding its muzzle shut, and scolding the dog. The problem with this form of discipline is that your dog will usually stop barking when you step outside, so it may not associate your actions with its negative behavior. The dog might even see barking as a way to get you outside with it.

If you want to solve the barking problem forever, don't reward your dog for excessive barking. Many owners just let the barking dog back into the home, without realizing they are playing into the dog's plan. It doesn't take the dog long to figure out that if it barks, you respond in the way it wants. Thus, the dog barks even more. And if you are not home to let the dog in, your neighbors will not be happy with you, and you could have some legal problems down the road.

Digging

Digging is often a dog's way of escaping boredom or making itself a cool place to nap. To stop this problem, you must catch the dog in the act. In a few cases a dog will stop digging forever if you simply scold it firmly a few times. But most of the time the temptation to dig is just too great, and when you have been out of sight and mind long enough, the dog will go back to work on its project.

133

As with barking, tins cans and the water gun are probably the most effective ways to deal with this problem. When you catch the dog digging, give it a dose of noise or spray of water. It will probably come to associate the negative action with its negative behavior and stop.

If you believe that your dog is digging because it is bored, then give it something to do. If outside toys don't work, then bring the dog inside with you.

Climbing on Furniture

It is best never to hold your puppy or dog on a couch, chair, or bed. If you do this, the dog will come to believe that it is welcome to get up there anytime. If you are home, you can order the dog down and scold it. This should end the problem. But what if your dog is making itself at home on your furniture when you are gone?

The best way to handle this problem is with newspapers and a few mouse traps. If your dog likes to sleep on the couch while your family is out, then set mouse traps on several spots on the couch and thoroughly cover the entire couch and the traps with newspapers. When your dog tries to climb onto the couch, the traps will go off, hitting the paper and making a great deal of noise. This will frighten the dog. It will not take very long at all for the dog to decide that it is better to sleep on the floor or in its own bed rather than on noisy furniture.

Exploring the Trash

With all the great smells that come from trash cans, is it any wonder that dogs are drawn to them? The easiest way to handle this problem is to have locking lids on your cans. If you don't or if your dog has figured out a way to knock the lids off, then use a mouse trap with a newspaper laid over it to scare the dog away. A well-fed dog will dislike the sound of a snapping trap more than it will be tempted by what is in the can.

A New Member of the Family

Some dogs have problems with a new baby. Many see this child as taking their place. Usually this passes very quickly, but there are ways to encourage a positive relationship between baby and dog.

First of all, make no change in the way you treat the dog. Don't give it any special attention, but don't ignore it, either. If the dog comes to realize that its place is secure, it usually will not feel threatened at all.

Don't put the child in the dog's face as a way of introducing them. If the baby suddenly moves or cries, the dog might be frightened and snap. You don't want this kind of greeting—it could scar both the child and dog for life.

Let the dog get to know the baby over a long period of time. Let the dog look at the baby through the bars of the crib while you are there. Let the dog watch as you rock the baby. Let it smell the baby's clothes or blanket. Let it become secure with its place and come to realize that the baby has a place, too. Over time, most dogs will become very protective of the new child and hover around anyone who is caring for the baby.

The most important thing is not to forget the dog. Don't hide the dog in a corner, make it feel unimportant or unloved, or push it away from the family. The dog needs to feel just as loved as before, or its behavior will change.

Some dogs stop eating if neglected when a new baby enters the family. Others forget their housebreaking training, begin to chew, or bark excessively. Usually all that is needed to fix any of these problems is a little positive attention and understanding.

A few dogs can't adjust. If your dog shows aggressive behavior to your new child and if time doesn't end this behavior, then you might have to part with the dog. This type of problem is discussed in chapter 14.

135

A Second Dog

If you bring a second dog into your family, don't just toss your new dog and old dog together. First let them get to know each other through a fence or gate. Watch them and keep them apart until it seems they are both reacting positively to each other. When you introduce them face-to-face, have both of them on a leash and be ready to pull them apart if they show signs of aggressiveness. Even after they have learned to get along, it is best not to feed them together for a while. If you don't push this relationship, it stands a much better chance of evolving into a solid friendship.

Many people wonder if a dog shouldn't have a say in whether or not your family gets another pet. No. If you have properly socialized your pet, it will not have a problem adjusting to your family's newest member.

Fleas and Ticks

Fleas and ticks are a part of life, but they can lead to health problems in both dog and family. You will not stop a flea and tick problem by simply getting rid of them on your dog. You must have a three-part plan of attack to rid yourself of these pests, and you must do these three steps on the same day if possible.

First, you must treat your yard. New products are being introduced all the time, and you will have many choices as to how to accomplish this. Make sure that the product you use will not harm your children or landscaping.

Second, treat your home. This is usually easier. There are sprays and foggers made for just this purpose.

Finally, treat your dog. In most cases a flea and tick collar will help and is a solid aid to combating the return of the pests, but a collar is not usually enough. A host of powders, sprays, shampoos, dips, and now even pills can help you make your dog a pest-free zone. If you brush your dog each day, you will be able to spot any pests as they appear and also figure out what products work best for your dog.

Your veterinarian will have access to the latest and best information concerning how to treat your dog. Before you attack the pests, talk with her.

Doggy Day Care

What to do with your dog when you are at work is a problem that is compounded by the fact that an unattended dog can get into a great deal of trouble. While there are more options than there were a few years ago, doggy day care is still a major problem for many families.

In several large cities there are actual day care centers for pets. Some dogs thrive in this type of environment; others don't. If you can afford the expense for someone to watch your pet while your family is at work and school, you might want to check your Yellow Pages and visit such a facility.

In many cities there are men and women who will come by once or twice a day to check on and exercise your dog. These animal nannies or dog walkers are cheaper than day care centers because they make the rounds of many homes each day. If your dog must go outside at least once during the day or if it gets very lonely, the visiting nanny might be a solution for you.

You can confine your dog to a small room at home or allow it to roam through the entire house. If you are gone for long periods of time and no one can come home and see the dog during the day, then be ready to confront a mess when you return. If you choose this route, it is best to have your dog paper-trained. It is also advisable to leave a radio or television on for company, and make sure there are toys and other activities to keep the dog from being bored. Also, most dogs like to be in a place where they can look out a window.

If you have a secure backyard, then your dog will be best left outside. Make sure that it has a place where it can be sheltered from the weather. Rain, snow, wind, and cold can take their toll on all dogs, especially those who spend most of their lives inside. Also, make sure your yard is secure from intruders. You don't want someone to leave your gate open and allow your dog to escape, and you don't want someone to be able to steal your dog.

The most important aspect of leaving a dog alone is making sure it has something to do. A puppy needs activities and toys, or it will begin to develop destructive habits such as chewing on everything in sight. An older dog might not have as great a need for toys as a pup, but it will need activities. Whether your dog is outside or inside, don't leave it alone with nothing to do. If you do, you will probably come home to chewed shoes or furniture, holes in your yard, or torn-up children's toys.

138

Remember, if a dog stays by itself, it will need water. To ensure that its water supply is adequate, make sure the bowl is large enough, cannot be tipped over, and is filled with clean water before you leave.

A Final Note

Many episodes of *Lassie* dealt with Lassie being bored while Timmy or Jeff was away at school. Because it was a different era and a rural setting, Lassie could relieve some of her boredom by roaming the woods, visiting with neighbors, and exploring open fields. Yet in her mind, no adventure compared to the joy of her owner coming home to be with her.

Today few dogs can roam, and hardly any should be allowed to. There are too many people and too much traffic. So the adventures a dog has when it is alone are very limited. This means a family has to plan for the times when a dog is by itself. Make sure your dog has toys or activities to keep it occupied; make sure it has water and food when it needs them; and make sure you have given the dog things to do that will keep it out of trouble. If your dogs digs or chews because of boredom, it is not the dog's fault.

Problems and Solutions

If you have a dog who is part of your family, seriously consider the option of doggy day care. In most cases when the dog is alone, it is counting the minutes until your family comes home. For the dog's sake and yours, make sure its time without you is as productive as you can make it.

Chapter 11

Special Opportunities, Skills, and Jobs

OUR DOG LADY HAS WORKED AS A THERAPY DOG FOR SEVEN YEARS. HERE SHE IS WITH HER BEST FRIENDS, RANCE AND CLINT.

For more than five decades Lassie has been the world's most famous dog. He has made many movies, had his own radio show, filmed hundreds of television episodes, endorsed thousands of products, and performed live at some of the top venues in the United States. Yet for Rudd and Robert Weatherwax, Lassie's most productive and satisfying work has taken place out of the camera's eye. In nursing homes, children's hospitals, orphanages, veterans' treatment centers, bond rallies, and schools, Lassie has touched hearts and lives one-on-one. This service-oriented work has made Lassie one of the most honored canines in dog history.

Several years ago, Rudd, Robert, and Lassie IV were filming outdoor scenes for the *Lassie* television series in the Great

Smoky Mountains. After shooting a very grueling segment in which Lassie had to charge up a mountain and negotiate a log bridge, the Weatherwaxes were taking their dog back to a trailer to rest. Just as they got to the film crew's camp, a woman approached them.

"Is Lassie your dog?" she asked Rudd.

"Yes, he is," Rudd proudly answered.

"My son watches *Lassie* every week," the woman explained, "and he and I read all the books. It has been his dream to actually get to meet Lassie. I apologize for bothering you. I know you must be very busy, but we drove several hours to get here, and it would mean the world to him."

Though Lassie was tired, and a great deal more was going to be demanded of him that day, Rudd nevertheless honored the woman's request. Rudd, Robert, and Lassie waited in the shade of a tree as the woman raced to an old station wagon. When the boy got out of the car, the Weatherwaxes realized he was blind. His face covered with a smile, he held on to his mother's arm as she led him back to Lassie.

Before mother and child got to them, Rudd motioned for Lassie to go forward and meet the boy. When the boy felt Lassie nudge his hand, he fell to his knees and threw his arms around the dog's neck. Then, very slowly, his hands carefully explored Lassie's face.

"Mom," he exclaimed after a few seconds, "Lassie is just as beautiful as I thought."

As Robert would later recall, it seemed as if Lassie could sense what was wrong with the boy and adapt to it. I have noted the same thing with most well-trained dogs. When they are around a fragile person, they are more gentle. When they are with someone with a disability, they seem to know how to respond. When they are with a person who has special needs, they not only react to those needs but seem to accept actions from these special people that they might not accept from someone else.

A few years ago I was with Robert Weatherwax and Lassie VII in a New York City bookstore. Robert allowed Lassie to roam freely from child to child and from aisle to aisle. Because of Lassie's training, Robert had complete faith that the dog would act appropriately in every case.

Part of the reward of having a dog is the joy of sharing it with others. If you socialize your dog, if it is well trained and exhibits good manners, it can do more than add joy to your family, it can be a friend to everyone your family touches.

The Skills

If your dog has been properly socialized, if it has learned its basic training and obedience work, then it might be ready to expand into special arenas and spotlights. The key for making this step is answering the question: "Do I have faith that we have done a good enough job with our dog so that we can trust it in every new and unpredictable venue?"

If you are to open the world to your dog, then your dog must be ready to meet that world. It must not be frightened of it, must not respond aggressively toward it, and must enjoy being there. You must also have such great control over your dog that its behavior or lack of discipline will not put it in danger. In new situations when you say, "Stay," it must immediately stay. If it doesn't, it might cost the dog its life.

Before expanding your dog's life to include one or all of the special opportunities that we will cover in this chapter, take your dog out into an unfamiliar situation and test its training and its socialization. How does the dog react to your commands? Is it sharp, focused, and always respectful and obedient? Will it still be attentive to you in new settings? Does it meet people well? Does it respond negatively to any kind of person? Is it aggressive toward other animals?

Every dog who can should become part of the larger world. We need them as ambassadors of goodwill for all canines. Yet it is best to start small. Let your dog grow into the challenges it will face. When it has proven itself to a few people, then add a few more.

Local Pet Shows

Local pet shows are usually run as part of fairs or community celebrations. Unlike AKC dog shows, local pet shows usually don't have very high standards. Most dogs are divided into a few groups by either age or size. Then the dogs are judged by how they behave, how cute they are, and what kind of tricks they can do. Most children love this type of competition because they get to show off their pets personally. Most local shows like to have kids lead their dogs and put them through their paces. These shows give the younger members of your family an opportunity to spotlight not only how much your dog knows but how much your child has learned, too. If your dog has learned all the basic skills of obedience training, it may just bring home a ribbon. At the very least it will make everyone in your family proud while giving your children a chance to gain confidence and maturity in a public forum.

143

The AKC Good Citizen

For many years the American Kennel Club was viewed as an elitist organization that dealt with only high-bred dogs. The AKC seemed to have little to offer regular dog owners and the mutts who lived in their homes. This image has been dramatically changed thanks to the AKC Canine Good Citizen program.

This certification is open to all dogs, purebred or not. To earn a good citizen title, your dog simply has to show that it knows and will respond to your saying *sit, down, stay,* and *come,* and that it will also behave politely around other dogs, accept a stranger petting and leading it, and be able to walk through a crowd on a leash. If your dog can do these things, then it can earn its CGC title. With this title not only can you take your dog many places that are closed to most animals, including some hotels and parks, but you can begin the process of applying for certification in several different dog therapy organizations.

To find out more about how to sign up to obtain a CGC and when and where your dog can prove its worth, write the AKC at Canine Good Citizen, 5580 Centerview Drive, Suite 200, Raleigh, NC 27606.

Dog Shows

If you have a registered purebred dog, should you show him? Your dog won't know, so this is a question that can be answered only by your family.

Dog shows are very time-consuming. They also require a great deal of travel, effort, and expense. Yet they can be very rewarding. If a knowledgeable breeder has judged your dog worthy of competition in the show ring, then you may want to explore the possibilities. You should begin this exploration by attending an area dog show. There you can see what is required of both the dog and the owner, get a feel for how judges grade your breed, and visit with those who are involved in showing their dogs.

Next you should get a copy of the rules and the standards. By reviewing them you can add to your knowledge and begin to see and understand what judges are searching for when they view a dog. You can also get a feel as to how much time it takes even a really good dog to earn a championship.

It is important to study your family's lifestyle. What do you and your children do on the weekend? Do you attend family gatherings, sports events, or religious services? Do your kids want to travel to dog shows several times a year? Can you afford the financial demands of showing your dog? There will be travel expenses, lodging, and meals.

Finally, look realistically at your dog and ask yourself if it would be happy doing show work.

If you do decide to enter the show ring with your family's dog, there are many rewards. First and maybe most important, you will make a lot of good friends who know a great deal about dogs. Your children will be exposed to new experiences and gain new insights, and if they work the ring, they will have an opportunity to earn the Junior Showmanship title. Your dog also has a chance to win trophies and ribbons that your family can display.

Don't charge off into this by yourself. Make this a family decision. If the adults are the only ones interested in the show ring, then think about waiting until the kids have left home. A dog should bring family members together, not take them in different directions.

145

Obedience Work

This requires less work than the show ring, but it is a very precise competition. Just because your dog knows all the obedience commands in this book does not mean it can easily earn its championship. At obedience trials your dog will be going against scores of other dogs who know the commands, too. In this competition you can lose points if your dog doesn't have perfect sitting form.

There are three levels of obedience trials: novice, open, and utility. If you decide to challenge for an obedience title, you will work your way through all three categories. The AKC spells out the specifics of the point system and rules, but to really understand how obedience trials work, your family needs to watch one. A trial is fascinating and exciting because it presents dogs that are judged on their intelligence and discipline. While some show dog champions compete and win their championships here, the number is few. Most obedience champions come from pet stock dogs.

One of the best things about obedience trials is that almost any dog can work hard enough to learn what is necessary to win a title. It may take time and effort, but it is possible. The other special point of this work is that the dog and the handler are a team. Therefore, the deeper the bond that a member of your family makes with your dog, the greater the chance for achieving the goal of a title. Best of all, the handler can earn special awards and honors, too.

An obedience title says a great deal about both your dog and your family. The award assures you that your dog is not only smart and well trained but also loyal to your family. From beginning to end, this award really is a family affair.

Field Trials

There are all kinds of trials for dogs of various breeds and types. Many even allow mutts and unregistered dogs. If your dog falls into one of these categories, you can show its stuff at one of these trials. How do you teach your dog to trail, point, herd, pull a sled, or retrieve game? The best way is to contact someone who specializes in a dog like yours and see how that person learned to teach his or her own dog. Usually a trainer can point you to classes in your area.

Hunting field trials include several different classes and tests. The scent trials are meant for dogs who have been bred to follow game by using their nose. Pointing trials are for dogs who point out game to hunters. There are also earth trials for dogs who dig out their prey, sight trials for dogs who see and chase game, and retrieving trials for dogs whose job is to bring game back to their masters. All of these are wonderful opportunities if your family owns a dog that was bred for some kind of hunting work. Taking your dog through a training course is the only way to tell if it has the ability to compete.

In the northern United States and Canada, sled dog events are becoming more and more popular. Those ignorant of these races picture only huskies and malamutes pulling a heavily laden sled. In truth, collies, German shepherds, and even poodles are often used as sled dogs. It seems that dogs from every breed love to pull things and race against other teams of dogs. There are events for just a single animal, too, so don't rule yourself out of this competition just because you don't own enough dogs for a whole sled team. If you are interested and live in a snowy part of the country, contact the International Dog Sled Racing Association. You can find them on the Internet or write to IDSRA, JC 86, Box 3380, Merrifield, MN 56465.

Herding Trials

Even if you don't own a herding dog, these trials are fascinating. Though usually associated with border collies, dogs from many different breeds compete in these trials. The goal is for each dog to herd a group of sheep from one point to another. Sometimes the dog receives directions from its owner; other times it works on its own. If you have a herding breed and live on a farm, you can train your dog to compete in these trials. There are many clinics, workshops, books, and videos that can teach you how to work with your family dog.

147

Sports

One of the newest and most popular dog and family team endeavors is sporting competition. Backyard activities such as catching Frisbees, chasing balls, running obstacle courses, and even shooting a basketball have now grown into organized competitions with prize money, trophies, medals, and ribbons. A few are even televised.

If your dog has a special talent, you can contact local dog clubs, the SPCA, the Humane Society, or even the chamber of commerce and check on the times and events in local shows. Most local show winners go on to compete at regional and national championships. Dogs that have won gold medals have performed at NFL halftime shows, on television variety and late-night programs, and at many local festivals and events.

Many winners have earned enough in appearance money to put family members through college. Others, such as Bud the basketball-shooting dog, have gone on to star in movies.

There are no limits on breed and size in these competitions, and no dog is judged by any standards of conformity or beauty. If you watch these dogs work—or should we say play?—you can see not only a great deal of talent but how much fun they are having. So if your family dog can catch a Frisbee or do gymnastic routines, sign it up. The world might just line up to watch and reward all of you for your efforts.

Raising Dogs for Special Service

Organizations that use guide dogs, dogs for the deaf, and dogs for the wheelchair-bound are always looking for families who will raise a puppy to adulthood, teach it specific commands and behaviors, and then turn the dog over to the organization to place with people with disabilities who need a dog to help them function in the world. This is noble and selfless work since your family would be required to invest a great deal of time and effort in a dog who will then be given away. Yet the rewards of knowing that your care, love, compassion, and guidance helped prepare a dog for such a special service may teach some of the most profound and meaningful lessons that a child could ever learn. Having a dog helps all of us learn a great deal about love and giving, and training a service puppy brings these lessons into focus in a unique way.

Dog Therapy

More and more family dogs are being used to help people heal. Registered therapy dogs work in children's hospitals, nursing homes, and schools every day. What do they do? They allow people to pet them, hug them, and love them. That is their only job.

There are many local and national dog therapy associations. Hospitals and nursing homes in your area will probably have their names and telephone numbers. If you have a dog that has a proven laid-back temperament and has earned its AKC Canine Good Citizen degree, you can probably qualify for a therapy certificate. With this certificate you can do volunteer work in your area.

While every program and opportunity covered in this chapter offers a great deal to your dog and your family, perhaps

LADY'S LICENSE FOR THERAPY DOGS INTERNATIONAL.

149

nothing teaches a child more than this program. Seeing the response of dying children on a cancer ward to a loving dog, watching an elderly person pet your family's dog, or being able to show schoolchildren how to properly handle a dog are special opportunities that will affect your child and you in some very special ways.

On one of our visits to a nursing home, our dog Lady, my ten-year-old son, and I were ushered into a dark room by the head nurse. She introduced us to a fragile woman in a wheelchair. As the elderly woman looked up, my son signaled for Lady to cross the room and lay her head in the woman's lap. As the woman petted the dog, she asked her name and remarked about how much she looked like Lassie. For several minutes, as she petted Lady, the woman told us about her family, her dogs, and the many times she had watched *Lassie* movies and television shows with her children and grandchildren. When we left the room, the nurse informed us that the woman had not spoken sensibly to anyone in almost five years. Petting Lady had awoken her memory and given her a chance to communicate with people again.

Several years ago, after months of weekly trips to local nursing homes, our dog Lady was awarded the Volunteer of the Year award by a local church group. At the banquet Lady happily accepted the special certificate and posed for the news cameras. Yet the award and the press coverage meant not as much to Lady or to us as the smiles on all those faces each week when Lady went to visit.

If you have a chance to do therapy work and if your dog is qualified, I highly recommend it. Your dog will love the chance to be the center of attention, and your children and you will gain a whole new appreciation of what it means to give. Dogs seem to live their lives always trying to give to us, and therapy work with our dogs teaches us to love freely and give openly like our dogs.

A Final Note

Growth is so important to all of us. If we lock ourselves and our dog in our homes and never venture out into the world, we will cease to grow. By participating in one or more of these programs, competitions, trials, or events, your family and your dog will benefit in many different ways. Don't miss the chance to put your family and your dog in a special spotlight.

Millions have dreamed of their dog being just like Lassie. The way to achieve that goal is to do what Rudd and Robert Weatherwax have done: help a dog learn, then share it with others.

Chapter 12

On the Road

When Pal, the first Lassie, landed the starring role in *Lassie Come Home*, he traveled to the shooting location in a train's baggage car and ate out of a bowl under a tree. When the movie became a smash hit, things changed a great deal. Suddenly Lassie was welcomed up front in the club car, could dine at the best restaurants, and was invited to most of the major motion picture premieres.

Today Lassie VIII goes almost everywhere Robert Weatherwax goes, and he still gets there in style. Lassie rides with Robert in cars, trucks, limos, and even in the first-class section of planes. He stays in the finest hotels, is welcomed at the best theaters, and rarely eats his meals outside unless he is in the mood for a picnic. Because he is so well behaved, traveling with Lassie is not much different from traveling with any other member of the Weatherwax family.

Lassie has earned the right to have the rules bent for him, but most dogs and their families face a different challenge when traveling. Family dogs can't ride the bus or train, some airlines don't want them, many motels and hotels refuse service to them, and some campgrounds and beaches have posted signs that say NO DOGS ALLOWED. Yet in spite of these difficulties, many families still want to take their dog with them when they travel. The good news is that if you have planned your trip well, there is no reason that taking a dog on a trip won't be a wonderful experience for your dog and your family.

Is Your Dog Ready for a Trip?

152

A dog cannot just hop in a car and take off across the country with you. You must be sure the dog can successfully make the journey. A trip to the vet will assure you that your dog is healthy enough to stand the stress of several days on the road; the vet can provide you with the paperwork and tags you will need to prove that your dog has obtained all the necessary vaccinations required by the places you are visiting. Your vet will also be able to advise you about what special medicines you should take with you and how to adapt your dog's diet to the sudden change in schedule, exercise, and location.

Next you will need to make sure your dog's manners are finely tuned. Your dog must be able to walk on a leash for long periods of time, sit and stay when asked, and be mannerly around other dogs, animals, and strangers. Your dog must not bark excessively and must be able to let you know when it needs to be taken out. If there are breakdowns in any of these areas, you might be in for a long, trying time.

Finally, you must be able to judge if your pet is going to be happy traveling with you. Most dogs are, but a few just don't do well when away from home. Before you try a long trip, it might be best to make a few all-day outings, then a short overnight or weekend excursion. If your dog manages these well and remains happy and healthy, then it will probably be able to take a trip for as long as any child.

Carsickness

Your dog can't take a vacation with you if it doesn't like to ride in a car, and many dogs don't. Because of carsickness, a few simply can't go on road trips. If your dog can't travel, then you will miss a lot of opportunities to have fun with it, so, if possible, help your dog get over its carsickness.

Most dogs who get carsick are simply reacting to fear and nervousness. They may fear a car because it took them away from their mother and siblings or because they associate it with going to the vet for shots or because they don't like the sound of a car engine. Rudd Weatherwax often treated this anxiety-related carsickness by taking his dogs for rides without ever leaving the driveway.

Rudd would grab his dog's favorite toy and invite the dog to play in his parked car. For several days he would repeat this process. Each day he and the dog would stay a little longer. When the dog had gotten comfortable with playing in the car, Rudd would turn on the radio. Once the dog got used to that, Rudd would let the engine idle. Eventually Rudd would take the dog on a two- or three-minute ride. He would follow this first ride with several more, each time a little longer in duration. In most cases the dog would lose its fear and nervousness by associating the car with something good. Rarely did a dog treated with this solution ever again get sick while riding.

What You Won't See

When you take your dog with you, your options are much more limited than when traveling without a pet. Many parks and motels, almost all restaurants, and most public tourist sites don't allow dogs except for those in service work, such as Seeing Eye dogs. This means that you need to check and plan carefully what you can do on your trip. You must call ahead, consult a travel agency, and talk with others who take their dogs on vacations. By doing your homework you can have a definitive plan and have something to do each step of the way.

There are amusement parks that accept leashed dogs, such as Silver Dollar City in Branson, Missouri, but most don't. There are many state and national parks that allow dogs in certain sections, but many ban them. Many motel chains will accept dogs if deposits are made or if they receive guarantees that the dog has been through obedience training and is housebroken, but others won't ever accept a canine. Many outdoor tourist sites, such as beaches and water resorts, also allow dogs, but you must check ahead. Because you can't take a dog everywhere, it will be up to you to find out the places that will accept your dog. As more dogs travel, more businesses are opening their doors to them. Don't turn your back on any options before you have checked them. A hotel may not have accepted dogs two years ago, but the owners might have changed the rules since they printed their last brochure. If you check the Internet or local bookstores, you will find information on where dogs are accepted in the areas you are traveling.

Because of state health laws, traveling with a dog means going through drive-throughs rather than dining in. You will spend most of your vacation eating in your car or at a picnic table. This is not bad if the weather is warm and sunny, but during rain, snow, and high wind, it can be a pain.

Finally, if you like to stop and visit out-of-the-way antique stores or craft shops, which means you would have to leave your dog in the car, you are advised not to travel with it. If the weather is warm, a dog can die of heatstroke if left too long in an automobile. Some cities have laws against leaving a dog in a car. Finally, scores of dogs are stolen out of cars each day.

Make sure that you can include your dog in the activities of your trip.

How to Travel

Lassie gets to travel first class on the airlines Robert Weatherwax uses; most dogs don't. If you have a small dog, an airline might allow you to carry it on board with you in a dog-carrying crate, but only if that crate will fit under your passenger seat. You will need to check airline regulations long before you plan your flight. If your dog is any larger than a toy breed, it must ride in the baggage compartment.

Many dogs cannot stand the stress of being locked in a crate and stored away in a remote section of a plane. The noise, the change in air pressure, and the sensation of actually being off the ground and in the air can create a great deal of stress. Many dogs have died during travel due to heart attacks brought on by this stress. If you must take your dog on a plane and are concerned that it might become extremely agitated, then you might want to have the veterinarian provide a sedative to calm the dog down.

The cost of transporting a pet with you or in the luggage compartment varies, but in general most airlines charge about $50 per trip. All airlines that take dogs must know well ahead of time that your dog will be on the plane. You will probably have to get to the terminal early and have your crate checked and securely fastened. If you are going to fly with your dog, plan the particulars well in advance.

Is it risky to take a dog on a plane? Though there is no one answer, there is a greater risk for dogs in flying than traveling by car. Airlines have been known to lose dogs. Dogs have been known to escape from crates. Some have not been unloaded at the right destination point, some have been exposed to great temperature extremes, and some have died from stress-related problems. On the other hand, many dogs travel often and well, and most animals who fly make it to their destination safely.

Most dog owners like to travel with their pets by car. A car offers a dog the chance to be with you, stretch its legs, relieve itself on a regular basis, and have the comfort of loved ones around it while having new experiences. In other words, it is far less stressful.

156

A dog should not be allowed to roam in a car. If you have room—and many vans and sport utility vehicles do—keep your dog in a crate. If this is impossible, then purchase a special dog seat belt attachment. This will not only keep your dog from roaming while the car is in motion and hold it in place in event of an accident, but it will also keep it from darting out an open door during a stop. Many dogs have been lost or killed by jumping out of a car and into traffic. No matter how prepared the owners thought they were, they couldn't react fast enough.

A good travel rule to follow is never to unbuckle your dog from a seat belt or let it out of a traveling crate until you have snapped its leash in place.

What to Take

When going on a trip there are a number of items you will need to pack for your dog. The list that follows contains only the necessities. Your dog may have special toys or bedding you should bring to make its trip less stressful.

- ID tags that show the telephone number of your veterinarian. If you are separated from your dog while on your trip, the tag will give the finder a way to identify your dog and call to let someone know it has been found.
- A luggage tag you can attach to your dog's collar that has a place to insert a card. Each time you stop for the night, write your name and the address and phone number of the place you are staying on the card and insert it in the luggage tag. If your dog gets lost, there is a local number for the finder to call and contact you.
- Two leashes. If you lose one, the backup can get you through the rest of the trip.
- Jugs of water from your tap at home and a water dish. Dogs have sensitive systems, and if you change water during a trip, your dog might get an unsettled stomach. Having a dog throw up in a car is not a pleasant experience. If you don't bring your own water, use bottled water.
- Rags, towels, a cleaning solution, a small bucket, plastic garbage bags, and a small shovel. Perhaps your dog will not get sick or have accidents, but you have to be prepared.
- Plastic bags and a small shovel to clean up and dispose of any messes your dog makes while relieving itself.
- A food bowl and enough dog food for the duration of the trip.
- A brush and other grooming aids.
- Any medication that your dog takes on a regular basis or that the vet has prescribed for the trip. You will also need your dog's first-aid kit. What goes in it is covered in chapter 13.
- Proof of vaccinations.
- A good flea powder or spray and a flea-killing shampoo in case you run into infested areas.
- A good flashlight for those night walks.

157

Where to Stay

The guidebooks for many national motel and hotel chains usually indicate those that take pets. But don't trust the guides entirely. Call ahead, check the rules and regulations, explain your situation, and make reservations for every stop of your trip ahead of time.

If you are camping, check to make sure that the campground allows dogs. Many do not. Some that do have certain regulations, such as a special fee or registration for each dog. Find out everything ahead of time. You don't want surprises.

Finally, check with your friends who travel with their dogs. They will know places to stay, eat, and visit, and will be glad to pass this advice along to you.

If You Leave Your Dog Home

There are a number of good reasons to leave your dog home: if the trip is an emergency, visiting areas that don't allow dogs, lack of space at your destination, or having to stay with someone who doesn't like or is allergic to dogs. If you must leave your dog behind, then carefully consider your options.

The best thing you can do for your dog is to have someone stay with it at your home. That way, its routine doesn't change and there is very little stress. If you have a friend who will sit for you, this is an excellent, almost worry-free option for both you and your dog.

If you cannot get a full-time sitter, then see if a dependable friend will check on your dog two or three times a day to help relieve boredom, give the dog fresh food and water, and let it go outside. You will need to leave a radio turned on to help keep the dog company and leave plenty of toys to keep it occupied.

In place of a friend, there are professional dog sitters who will stop by and take care of your dog's needs each day. These men and women will not be able to spend as much time with your dog, and their care will probably not be as loving as that of a close friend. Still, their living depends on your being satisfied with their work, so you can usually trust them.

Dog swapping can be a positive experience if you have friends who will take care of your dog at their house in exchange for your doing the same for them when they are gone. For this to work, your dog must understand the rules of your friends' home, get along with them and their pets, and feel comfortable in their house.

Most vets board animals. As your vet will know your dog, this is a pretty safe choice, but if you are on a tight budget, it can be costly. Many kennels also board outside animals. If you are close to the breeder from whom you bought your dog, then he might help you out. When boarding at a vet or a kennel, make sure that your dog will receive good care, have a comfortable place to stay, and get daily exercise and attention.

No matter where you keep your pet, make sure that the person you leave in charge knows what to do if your dog gets sick or injured. Don't expect the person caring for your dog to pick up the bill on faith. Work out a payment plan ahead of time with your vet.

A Final Note

Most dogs love to travel. They enjoy the adventure of seeing new places and meeting new people as much as you do. Most families enjoy having their dogs with them. Children especially love having a friend to fill the long hours on the road and a playmate to help pass the downtime. Yet as was often presented on the *Lassie* television shows, traveling with your dog offers special problems and dangers. There is no excuse for not being prepared. Check ahead so that you can assure yourself of a vacation that is as trouble-free as all family vacations should be.

Chapter 13

What's Up, Doc?

One of the most memorable characters on the original *Lassie* television series was Doc Stuart. This country vet was not only a regular visitor to the Miller and Martin farms but treated Lassie for snakebites, broken bones, deafness, head injuries, and countless diseases. Once, when Timmy was very ill, Lassie thought so much of Doc Stuart that she got him to come and look in on her master.

While it is true that the man who played Doc Stuart was just an actor and that Lassie was also just playing a part, the relationships presented among dog, family, and doctor were ones that your own family should try to emulate. Your vet usually works long hours, faces a wide variety of complex problems daily, and never once gets to ask his or her patients what is hurting. Will Rogers once said, "If I am really sick, take me to a vet. If he can figure out what is wrong with my dog, then I am sure he will know how to treat me." Outside of your family, this is the most important person your dog will ever know.

Having a good relationship with a veterinarian is one of the most important things you can do for your dog. From time to time your dog's life will be in your vet's hands. If your vet knows you and your dog well, if you have kept your appointments and made sure your dog has had its annual checkups, the good doctor will always be one step ahead in treating your dog. So it is very important that the doctor you choose not only know veterinary medicine well but is a person with whom you can talk openly and honestly about anything that has to do with your dog's behavior or health.

I think it is very important for children to go to the veterinarian's office with one of their parents and the dog. Having family members along will help soothe and calm your dog, and will also give your children a relationship with the professional who is in charge of their dog's health. Then, if your dog has a medical emergency while you and your spouse are not at home, your children will know whom to call to get advice or help.

Preparing for a Visit to the Vet

Your puppy or dog must be easy to examine in order for your veterinarian to do a thorough job of checking it from head to tail. To ready the dog for the visit, lift it up on a table, check and examine its paws, open its mouth and look down its throat, and examine both ears. If your puppy gets used to being handled in this way by members of its family, it will be much easier for it to be a good patient at the doctor's office.

Before you go to the vet for a regular visit, make sure your dog is clean. A clean dog will be easier to check for external parasites, skin problems, and other signs of distress or disease.

Finally, don't take a dog to the veterinarian's office if you don't have the proper equipment for controlling your animal. You never know the people and animals you are going to meet when you open the waiting room door. (I once discovered a full-grown cougar on a leash waiting to be examined.) Keep your dog on a lead so that you will be able to handle any situation that might arise.

General Care Visits

Puppies will visit a vet several times in their first year of life. The reason for these multiple visits is that vaccinations are given at a lower dosage than those given to an adult dog, so the period of time they protect your puppy is less. Once a dog reaches the age of one, unless it has been injured or becomes sick, it should require only one visit per year.

Puppies and dogs are vaccinated against several different diseases. The best-known vaccination is for rabies, a viral disease that is always fatal in animals. It can be passed to your dog by other dogs, cats, skunks, raccoons, rats, and many other animals. If a human is bit or scratched by a rabid animal and does not receive the necessary treatments, he or she will die. Even if you think your dog has no contact with other animals, you must keep your rabies shots current.

Most vets inoculate against infectious canine hepatitis. This disease also is a killer, and dogs who do manage to survive are usually disabled in some way. It is always advisable to receive this shot as well.

Leptospirosis is an almost always fatal disease that causes kidney and liver problems. It can be transmitted from dog to dog or from dog to human. Though not often fatal in humans, it can cause kidney and liver disease, such as jaundice.

Parvovirus is highly contagious. This disease hits quickly, zapping your dog of all its energy. If you are familiar with feline distemper, then you understand the fatal results of this disease. Parvo, as it is most commonly called, can be prevented. If your dog is going to be around other dogs at shows, kennels, or in public places, it should probably get this shot.

Bordetella, also known as kennel cough, can also be prevented by a shot. While this disease does not always mean death, it is one that should be avoided.

The other major killer of unvaccinated dogs is canine distemper. Few dogs have survived an attack of distemper, and those that do rarely return to top form. This is a horrible killer and crippler, and it doesn't have to be. Make sure your dog is inoculated each year.

In an age when shots can be so easily administered and these six diseases can be so easily prevented, it is a shame for any dog to die from one of them. Just as you need to immunize children to prevent polio and other illnesses, remember to keep your dog's shots up to date, too. Dogs are required to be vaccinated to protect themselves, humans, other pets, and native wildlife. Besides the fact that you are helping to keep your dog well, you are also complying with the laws of your city, county, and state.

In many areas a combination shot is given to an adult dog to protect it for three years. Some states and cities do not allow this long-term shot and require a dog to be seen and licensed annually. Your vet will know the local laws and will be able to tell you what type of shots are best suited to your dog.

Finally, make sure to keep all vaccination records where they can be retrieved easily. If your dog should bite someone and you cannot prove it has been vaccinated, it will have to be put to sleep so that authorities can perform an autopsy to determine if it has rabies. Without proof of inoculation, there is no other recourse.

Worms

The mere thought of worms disgusts many people, yet it is a fact that all puppies are born with them. Having worms in their system at birth jump-starts their antibodies. Yet by the time a puppy is eight weeks old, it doesn't need worms anymore.

163

Before you bring a puppy home that is more than eight weeks old, ask if it has been wormed. If it has, have your vet worm her again at twelve weeks. Otherwise, worm the puppy immediately, then schedule a second treatment for a month later.

Dogs of all ages can get worms. The most deadly are heartworms; other types include whipworms, tapeworms, roundworms, and hookworms. Your vet can find all of them except heartworms by examining your dog's stool, so bring a fresh sample with you in a sealed plastic bag. If worms are discovered, the vet will give your dog medicine to eliminate them.

Heartworms are passed to a dog by mosquitoes. Until 1997 they were untreatable; a dog that got heartworms died in a matter of months or years. Now, thankfully, there is an effective treatment if the worms are caught early, but the best way to handle this problem is with a monthly pill that prevents heartworms altogether. Your vet should test your dog for heartworms at each annual checkup.

Many veterinarians can now offer you a pill that not only prevents heartworms but stops fleas, too. Taken once a month, this new development in pest prevention is positive news for dogs and families.

The topic of fleas and ticks was addressed in chapter 10. It is enough to say here that to control them you must eliminate them from your dog, your home, and your property.

Beyond Regular Checkups

Many families have a problem knowing when their dog is sick. If you live with your dog, work with it, feed it daily, play with it, and brush it, then you should be able to note a change in its behavior that tells you it is not feeling well. Here are some other signs of possible illness:

Vomiting
Loss of appetite

Fever
Diarrhea
Constipation
Blood in stool or urine
Loss of weight
Runny nose
Watery eyes
Coughing
Areas sensitive to normal brushing or petting
Excessive whining
Foul breath
Sour odor from mouth or body
Skin lesions
Listlessness
Weakness in limbs
Excessive sleeping
Dramatic change in personality
Bumps or knots on the body

If you note one or more of these conditions and it lasts more than one day, you will need to visit your vet. Don't delay. If your dog does not receive treatment quickly, it will cost more later and the treatment may be too late.

Mild Diarrhea or Indigestion

Loose stools that last a day or less are probably not a problem. If the condition is minor, you might want to try a dose of an over-the-counter medication your family uses for upset stomach or diarrhea. Adjust the dose to the size of the dog. Chewable tablets might be easy for you to administer. If your dog's condition has not improved after twenty-four hours, call your veterinarian's office. Ask if you should bring your dog to the office or if you need to come in to pick up medication.

Cuts and Scrapes

If the cut is small, you can treat it yourself. The best way to assure that the area is properly treated is to trim the hair around the wound, clean the area with hydrogen peroxide on a cotton ball, then coat with an antibiotic cream that you use on your children.

If the cut is deep and long, apply pressure to slow the bleeding, wrap with gauze, then tie with a clean rag or cloth. If the dog cannot walk, pick it up by placing your arms just in front of its front legs and just behind its back legs, then rush the dog to the vet. If it is after hours, contact your veterinarian at home or drive to an emergency veterinary clinic.

Burns

Burns are serious. Even a minor burn can lead to infection. For emergency treatment smear the area with petroleum jelly, then take your dog to the vet.

Choking

If something gets caught in your dog's throat and it can't seem to breathe, you will need to do something quickly. First pry open its mouth, shine a flashlight down its throat if you have one handy, and see if you can tell what is causing the problem. If you can see it, reach in with your hand and try to pull it out. If you can't see it or can't pull it out, then try putting your arms around your dog's stomach, just behind the rib cage, and give a quick thrust. If after two or three attempts the object will still not dislodge, then rush the dog to your vet.

Poison

If you even think your dog may have ingested poison, you must react quickly. Force either a strong mixture of saltwater or a fifty-fifty mix of hydrogen peroxide and water down the dog's throat. This should make it vomit. Then rush the dog to the veterinarian, if possible bringing along the container that held the poison.

Limping

A dog with a minor limp usually has cut the pad of its paw or has something stuck in its pad or between its toes. Don't worry if there seems to be a lot of bleeding in these cases; feet tend to bleed more heavily than other body parts. Look for a cut and check to see if an object is still lodged in the paw. If you find something, use tweezers to pull it out. If the cut is not large or deep, clean it, bathe it in hydrogen peroxide, and then allow it to heal naturally. Until the wound is completely healed, continue to disinfect it each day to prevent infection.

167

Insect Stings

Most dogs take an insect sting better than most people. They also quickly learn to avoid the bug that hurt them. If a stinger has remained embedded, remove it with tweezers. You probably will have no more problems.

Some dogs are allergic to insect stings. Watch for breathing trouble, disoriented behavior, swelling in the eyes, or heavy coughing. If your dog shows any of these signs, take it to your vet or emergency care clinic immediately.

Allergies

Some dogs have allergies. There are treatments, but your vet will have to determine just what is causing the problem. Signs of allergies are watery eyes, skin problems, rashes, discharge from the nose, and sneezing. If your dog's allergies are not causing great discomfort or affecting its health, the dog and your family can probably live with them. If they are serious, consult your vet.

Artificial Respiration

Smoke inhalation, electric shock, drowning, falls, or being struck by a car can cause your dog to stop breathing. If the dog is not getting enough oxygen, its gums and tongue may turn blue, its chest may stop moving, and it may register shock in its eyes. If you find your dog in this condition, place it on its side, open its mouth, and clean away any obstructions to its breathing. Clean its nose, close its mouth and hold it closed with your hand, then take a deep breath, cover your dog's muzzle with your mouth, and exhale into the dog's nose. If you are doing this properly, the dog's chest will rise. Remove your mouth, let the dog's chest deflate, take another breath, and repeat your action. You will need to set a pace at which you administer ten to fifteen breaths a minute. If possible, continue your artificial respiration while you have someone drive you and the dog to the vet. Don't stop giving treatment until your dog begins to breathe on its own.

In the case of a drowning, clear the lungs of water before you begin mouth-to-muzzle therapy. You can do this by holding your dog upside down by the back legs and letting the water run out of its lungs. Then begin according to the instructions above.

CPR

If your dog's heart is not beating, you can administer cardiopulmonary resuscitation. While one member of your family attempts artificial respiration, with the dog on its side, place the heel of your hand on its chest but behind the front leg's elbow. Place your other hand on top of your first hand and press down firmly, holding for two counts. Wait one second and then repeat. Your goal will be to give about twenty pumps per minute. If the dog begins to breathe and its heart begins to beat, you should stop. Of course your dog will need to see a vet immediately, who will determine the damage.

168

Serious Injury

If a dog has been seriously injured, you will need to transport it to an emergency care facility or your vet's office as quickly as possible. For head injuries, broken bones, deep cuts, and other traumatic concerns, be aware that your dog will be in shock and will probably not react as you would expect. It might even snap at you. It is wise to use a belt, cloth, or leash to muzzle the dog (tie its mouth shut) to keep it from biting you or a member of your family.

Giving Medication

The proper way to give a pill is to pry your dog's mouth open, then place the pill on its tongue at the back of the throat. Close its mouth, hold it closed, then either pat its head or rub its throat. Let go when you feel the dog swallow. Even after you think it has gotten the pill down, watch the dog for a few minutes to make sure it doesn't spit the pill out.

The best way to give liquid medicine is with a large eyedropper. Simply squirt the liquid into the side of the dog's mouth, placing the end of the dropper as close as you can to the back of the throat. If necessary, hold the dog's mouth shut to prevent it from spitting the liquid out.

Your First-Aid Kit

You should maintain a first-aid kit that contains things especially for your dog. Keep hydrogen peroxide and antiseptic cream for your dog's cuts and scratches; children's aspirin to give if your dog has a high fever; a diarrhea medicine; scissors; bandages; gauze; an eyedropper; and an animal eye wash. You should also have a rectal thermometer and lubricating jelly to coat it. Keep a record of your dog's normal temperature—commonly around 101 degrees Fahrenheit—written inside the kit.

Care of the Aging Dog

Your dog will give your family years of joy and excitement, never seeming to age. Then one day you will notice that your pet is moving a bit slower or limps when it gets up in the morning. When this happens, it will begin to dawn on everyone that the dog is now a senior citizen. Is the dog different now? Have its needs changed?

First of all, when your dog slows down, ease off on your demands. Make sure that young children understand they have to treat the dog more gently. Let the dog sleep a little longer, take a few more naps, or go to bed a bit earlier. It is still important to exercise the dog, but take shorter walks and slow the pace. Try to keep from changing too much in your dog's world because the animal will be much more comfortable if its environment stays the same. You also might want to consider putting your pet on a special diet for older dogs. Consult your veterinarian.

The older dog is more susceptible to cold, so make sure it has a warm place to sleep. Give the dog a thick pad or blanket and find a way to let it rest in the warmth of the sun or a fireplace. Realize that it may have less control over its bladder and bowels, so it will need to go out more often. If it makes a mistake, cut the dog some slack. It isn't the dog's fault. It is probably even more distressed about the mistake than you are.

The dog may no longer like to meet strangers and may even seem cranky around the family. Its eyes may not be as sharp, and its hearing may diminish as well. Thus it may become confused and bark at things that never bothered it before. Arthritis will probably set in, but there is now medicine that can help ease its stiffness and pain. Check with your veterinarian.

Your dog has given you the best years of its life, and as long as it is not so diseased that it is in great pain or misery, it can still spend some good days with you and your family. It is now time for your family to give back selflessly to your pet. Go out of the way to make it comfortable. Make your dog feel special. Constantly show how much it is loved. Spend quality time with your dog.

The lessons your children can learn from helping your dog in its old age can be just as important as what they learned from the dog when it was a puppy. The dog will help them to understand how to treat and respect not only older dogs but older people as well. By not fearing or avoiding the dog, by seeing it as it is and recalling how it was, by helping it each step of the way, the whole story of life will be played out for each member of your family. This will be the last lesson your family's dog can teach you, and it may just be the most meaningful and important.

Chapter 14

Tough Life-and-Death Decisions

J.D., ONE OF
THE BEST
DOGS I WILL
EVER KNOW.

One of the toughest jobs a family ever faces is parting with their dog. Saying a final good-bye to your best friend is one of the hardest things you will ever do.

In the mid-1960s, the producers of *Lassie* decided it was time to find Lassie a new master. CBS thought it was in the best interest of the series to take the show in another direction. As a way to keep Lassie but write out the Martin family, writers opted to have Lassie's television family move to Australia. Because of quarantine laws, the Martins could not take their dog with them. Faced with a hard decision, Timmy gave Lassie to a kindly neighbor. In the final episode with Jon Provost, June Lockhart, and Hugh Reilly (the actors who played the Martin family), Lassie didn't understand why she had been left with a neighbor. When she returned to her old home and found her family gone, she was confused and sad. Those who loved her were no longer where they should have been.

Of course Lassie was just playing a part that would pave the way for the show to revolve around the character's work with the United States Forestry Service. In truth, when the final bit of filming was completed, Lassie as always went to his real home with Rudd Weatherwax. Yet even though Lassie's home life remained a constant and he quickly bonded with the show's new actors, for a long time Lassie missed Jon, June, and Hugh.

Dogs develop bonds. These bonds run very deep. A dog learns not only to love its family but its home and everything in it. When a family member leaves, a move is made, there is a dramatic change in schedule, or another pet disappears from the home, your dog will usually display confusion and sadness. It is a normal facet of its being and one of the elements that makes the dog such a wonderful pet. Because its family and everything about it means so much to your dog, having to part with the dog can be a problem.

173

In this chapter we'll talk about what happens when unions must dissolve. These are some of the hardest moments in the lives of a dog and family, but if handled properly, they can also teach profound lifelong lessons.

What If It Doesn't Work Out?

There are several reasons why families may have to give up their dog. Some of the problems can center on the dogs themselves; others on the family. To begin to understand how to place a dog who can no longer stay in your home, first you must examine why your family is thinking of giving him up.

In some cases it is the dog who is at fault. In deciding the right way to deal with parting with a dog who can't mesh with your family, first look at the reasons that it doesn't fit in your home.

Does your dog have psychological problems that you cannot seem to resolve? This can be the case in dogs that have been inbred, mistreated, or abused before adoption or are the product of puppy mills. The best way to work through one of these problems is to talk with your vet first. The vet might be able to suggest some type of training that can help your dog or might know of another home where your dog would thrive. If your health professional feels that neither of these two options should be attempted, then you might want to talk about the possibility of having to put the dog down. Under no circumstances should you consider this if there are any other options available. There are a few dogs who are too confused to bond with anyone, but most problems can be fixed. Before you give up on your dog, work with your vet and other dog professionals to see if they can help your dog. The bond that might develop as you discover ways to help your dog deal with past traumas might teach a lesson to everyone in your family about working with people who have special problems as well.

Sometimes a family's dog will suddenly become mean, aggressive, and dangerous. This can happen in even a loving environment. Past abuse or in some cases disease or injury can radically change a dog's personality. If your dog becomes a danger to your family or others, then you should remove it from your home. If your vet believes your dog will never lose its aggressive tendencies and is a threat to society, then you may have no choice but to have your health professional put the dog down.

Your dog might develop allergies to grass, plants, food, and other common things around your home. If your vet determines that your dog's allergies are related to your home or yard, you have very few options. You can attempt to eliminate the problems and try medications. If these options do not work, then you will have to find a home for your dog where it will not be faced with the things that cause its sickness. If you take your dog to a shelter, please make sure to give the reasons for its having to leave your home. With this information they may be better able to place the dog.

Your dog might grow up and simply not be suited for your environment. In most cases this should have been foreseen before adopting the puppy, but sometimes people are forced to move to a smaller home and the dog is too large or possesses too much energy for the small home and yard. What you have to do then is find a home where the dog can thrive. If you can't move, then check with friends and family, leave a note at your vet's office, or run an ad in the newspaper. A shelter should be your last option. Don't ever dump your dog. It is against the law; it is cruel; and it usually results in the dog's being killed.

Your dog may have gotten out of your home or yard and then damaged a neighbor's property. In this case the dog might be forced out of your home because of a legal ruling. Once again, look for a friend or neighbor who can adopt your dog, check with a vet, or run an ad. As always, a last option is giving the dog to a shelter.

175

The Family

In many cases it isn't the dog who is responsible for a family having to give it up. Situations often change in family life that force families to consider parting with their pet.

Because of changes in schedules, jobs, school, or family health problems, your family might find itself without the time to take care of your dog. If this is the case, before making plans to dissolve the relationship, consider whether your lack of time is a temporary situation. If your family will have the time necessary to fully look after your dog a month or two down the road, then try adapting for a short period. Your dog will wait for you, and if you plan carefully, it will be in good shape when your schedule slows down. If you determine that your family is never going to have the time to properly care for your dog, then you must find a way to place your dog somewhere else. All options should be considered, including asking family and friends, taking out an ad, having your children talk to their schoolmates, calling the person who sold you the dog, or, as a last resort, taking the dog to a shelter.

Families sometimes have to move to a home or area where their dog cannot live. If this is the case, then the standard options of finding a new home must be used.

Some family members develop allergies to pets. If medication doesn't work, then your options are few. Some families simply make the dog an outdoor resident. In the right environment, this is not a bad option. If you don't have this choice, then you will have to find your dog a new home.

Some dogs cannot adjust to a new family member. If you have a new child and the dog cannot adapt, or if a grandparent moves in and your dog does not accept him or her, then you are faced with the prospect of having your dog disrupt your family. Since your family must come first, seek professional training for your dog. If this can't be done, then you will have to find it a new home.

When a financial strain hits a family, the cost of having a dog may be too great. If this is the case, you might have to give up the dog. Once again, seek a good home through your circle of friends and family.

There Are Few Easy Answers

Having to part with a dog is a trauma that offers few easy solutions. If your dog is still a puppy, if it is a member of a popular breed, and if you have trained it so that it is the envy of your neighborhood, then placement will probably be fairly easy. If the dog is not well behaved or has special problems, then it will be much more difficult to match the dog with the home it needs. Yet even in these cases it is usually possible to find a new home for the dog.

For your dog and family's sake, don't give up too soon. Your dog is a member of your family and deserves every consideration. If the dog is special to your family, it can be special to another family as well. Seek out every possibility, talk with all your friends, be honest, be straightforward, and let others see your true love for your dog. This will help you find it a home where you can be sure it will be loved and well taken care of.

Finally, a shelter is an option, but it should be your last one. This is not to say that shelters are horrible places. Most aren't. But these facilities are filled with animals that have been found on the street, have been dumped by uncaring owners, are members of unwanted litters, or have been brought in by people who didn't think or plan before they decided to get a pet. Shelters have a great deal of work to do with the thousands of cases they see each year. This means their ability to deal with your dog is going to be compromised by all the other work that has been forced on them. If you must take your dog to a shelter, consider one that has a no-kill policy. Then you can at least take comfort in the knowledge that your dog will not be put down after only a few days at the shelter.

177

Dealing with a Sick or Dying Dog

One of the realities of having a dog is knowing that at some point it will die. If it expires peacefully of old age in a quiet corner of your home or yard, your family's grief might be great, but this kind of death is often a blessing. Real trauma comes when the family has to decide when to put a very sick or dying dog out of its misery.

The Older Dog

If your dog has been a part of your home for years, you will be able to sense when things aren't right. If the dog is in constant pain, if it no longer seems to care about anything, if its eyes no longer shine, if it cannot control its bodily functions, if it has grown extremely moody, if it seems unhappy, or if it has gone blind or deaf, then you might have to help put it out of its pain, confusion, and embarrassment. This call will be your family's and your vet's. Together you must decide when it is time for your best friend to leave this world.

This decision shouldn't be easy. It should take a lot of study and thought. The problems of aging can often be addressed in a satisfactory manner through medication or a change in diet. Many dogs who lose their sight or hearing can still function in their homes and live many more productive years with only a little extra help from family members. In some cases bringing a new puppy or younger dog into your home will inject new life into an old veteran. In other words, just because your dog is old and not as strong as it once was may not be a reason to put it down. It has been your friend for life, so examine all the possibilities before deciding that its best days are behind it.

A Very Sick Dog

Though few like to talk about it, sometimes the cost of treating a dog is too high for an average family to afford. If your dog could be treated successfully with surgery or special medications but you cannot cover the cost, talk to your health professional. Find out if payment plans can be arranged or if there are special funds or grants that could help your family out. You may want to look into purchasing pet health insurance to avoid this possible problem. For a few dollars a month you might be able to assure treatment for your dog in the future.

Your vet will be able to help you decide if you need to put a very ill dog down. Sometimes cancer and other diseases so ravage a dog that the answer is clear. You will know when the dog is in too much pain and won't get well again. Yet making the decision to end its life is still a painful one. Before putting your dog to sleep, talk with everyone in your family, explain the situation and the options, and weigh everyone's opinion. If some are against it, then have them spend some time with the dog, have them talk to your vet, and then let them voice all their concerns in a family meeting. Since your dog has been part of your family, the whole family must be involved in this final act of compassion.

Putting Your Dog to Sleep

It is best if you don't desert your dog when it is being put down. Many vets allow families to be with their pet when it is being injected with the drug that will end its pain and suffering. If you stand by your dog, pet it, speak to it, comfort it, give it your love one last time, its distress will be less severe. It will be hard for your family to let go, but the experience may help prepare them for the future loss of a family member or friend.

179

A mother and father will know if their children can handle watching the family dog die. If your children are going to be with your dog when it takes its last breath, prepare them. Let them know why this has to happen and help them see the good in this moment. Let each child talk to the vet. Tears will flow and there will still be questioning, but at least the children will have a foundation already built to help hold the pain in their grieving hearts.

One Dog's Devotion

Almost twenty years ago my wife, Kathy, and I owned a wonderful German shepherd named J.D. He was one of the smartest, most devoted dogs I have ever known. We raised him from the time he was three months old, and over the years he developed the largest repertoire of tricks of any dog I have ever had.

When J.D. was four, he got sick. Our vet, Dr. Roy Young, discovered cancer. We tried new treatments, blood transfusions, and medicines, but nothing worked. After several long weeks of fighting, Kathy and I both knew that J.D. was never going to recover. We talked to Dr. Young about options, and when we discovered that there were none, we made an appointment to have our dog put to sleep the next day.

I slept on the floor with J.D. that last night. I brushed him, hugged him, and tried to explain what we were going to have to do. As he studied me with his big brown eyes, I felt at a complete loss as to how to say good-bye to this animal who had meant so much to me.

The next morning I carried him out to my car. Now fragile, his bones seeming to all but push through his skin and his hair falling out in bunches, J.D. still maintained the proud and noble spirit that had made him so special to us.

I was praying that we could walk right into Dr. Young's office and have J.D. immediately put to sleep. I didn't believe I could stand to wait. As it turned out, another dog had just been brought in that had been hit by a car. My wife, J.D., and I were forced to sit for fifteen minutes in the waiting room while the veterinary staff administered emergency treatment to the injured dog.

Dogs always seem to sense when people are upset. On this day J.D. knew that something was bothering me. Even though he was extremely weak, even though he had practically no white blood cells left in his body, our tan-and-black shepherd struggled to his feet one final time. Moving to a spot right in front of me, he went through his favorite tricks once more. His body was unsteady, his voice was weak, and he moved ever so slowly, but his face still lit up when I tearfully whispered, "Good boy," and patted his head. A few minutes later, after Dr. Young had once again confirmed that there was nothing else we could do, I stroked J.D.'s massive head for the final time and let him go.

I still mourn when I remember that moment. Thinking of that great dog trying to comfort me still brings tears. At first I thought my tears and heartache were caused by the decision to put J.D. to sleep. I thought I had somehow let him down and blamed myself. Over time I came to recognize that my pain was so great only because the joy of bonding with our dog had been so wonderful and meaningful. In his life J.D. taught me just how deeply a dog can love its family, and through his death I found out just how much that gift meant.

This book is all about the blessings that come from having a family bond with a dog. In most cases the bond between family and dog will remain intact until death. Though we may not want to think about it, we all know that death may not be fair, but it is a reality. Giving up a loved one is never easy. And if the bond is strong, saying a final good-bye shouldn't be easy. The decision of when your dog will die may fall to you. If it does, do what is right for the dog at the time. Don't be selfish, don't be ashamed, and don't be scared. If at all possible, be there for him as a family, be there with him, and thank him one last time for all that he has given to each of you.

Chapter 15

A Closing Charge

TODAY'S
LASSIE
CARRIES ON
A PROUD
TRADITION.

*I*n 1954, when producer Bob Maxwell and Rudd Weatherwax first formed a partnership to bring a Lassie television show to CBS, Rudd asked that a few guidelines be put in place for the series. If these guidelines were not met, then the trainer wanted no part of it.

First, Rudd demanded that each episode be written like a generic Sunday school lesson. He wanted every show to teach something special that could make families stronger. He asked for this because he saw a dog's most important family role as that of a teacher of important life lessons.

Second, he wanted the writers, directors, and producers to understand that Lassie should be asked to do only things a real dog could do. He didn't want Lassie to play superdog; he didn't want him to talk or be able to read. He wanted Lassie to represent what any well-trained dog could be.

Finally, Rudd asked that the image of Lassie never be tarnished. He wanted Lassie to represent the best qualities of the canine world. The trainer knew that if Lassie held true to this, he would always hold up an ideal for not only dogs but for families too.

Over the last fifty-plus years Lassie has not deviated from the course that Rudd first mapped out. On television and in motion pictures, Lassie has always represented a real dog doing things a real dog could do and, in the process, taught important lessons of life.

If Lassie is special, it is not because he is a collie or has been a major star for six decades. If Lassie is special, it is because he has brought to life the qualities that all dogs have the potential to bring to their own families.

If you use the wisdom of Rudd and Robert Weatherwax, your family will not only have a chance to capture the essence of Lassie in your own dog but also bond with a friend that will change your lives for the better.

Lassie's mantle can now be passed along to your family dog. It will be up to you to use these Lassie training methods and to expand their scope as well. Your dog can be a vital part of your family but only if you work to make it a reality.

Good luck!

Appendix

The Name Game

For many families, naming a dog is more trying than housebreaking or obedience training. It sometimes seems impossible for an entire family to settle on just one name. In some cases a dog will do something that ends the debate, creating an image that stands out so firmly that its name will be obvious. I have known dogs named Tip because as puppies they tipped over their food bowls. I once met a dog named Tripod because he had lost a back leg just weeks after birth. In many families, dogs are given the name of a favorite dog from the family's past. This passing of the torch makes picking a name easy. Yet with most dogs and puppies there is no clear-cut choice.

In the case of Pal, he became Lassie because the role he played in a movie grew into a full-time job. Each of the following generations of Pal's offspring also began life with a name that fit its puppy personality. Each dog became Lassie when he passed his exams and took over the starring role on television. Such was also the case with Rin Tin Tin and many other movie dogs.

What you name your dog will probably stick for its whole life. Give it some thought. Have your family suggest a number of different names. Write each one down in your doggy dictionary, and once you settle on one, stay with it.

For those who need some help, on the next few pages are some names from history and of entertainment's most famous dogs, as well as a few standard dog handles that just seem to work for every generation. If you would like even more dog names, check out Lynne Hamer's *Name That Dog*. Her book covers stories of the dogs of the world's most famous historical figures and personalities and features many rare photos. The book can be ordered by calling 215-692-5905 or writing Animal Press, 700 Bradford Terrace, West Chester, PA 19382.

Ace: crime-fighting hound from *Batman* comic books.

Adjutant: supposedly the world's longest-living dog. He died at twenty-seven.

Adonis: an English setter that was America's first registered dog.

Apollo: one of the Dobermans from *Magnum, P.I.*

Arnold: the dog from *Life Goes On.*

Asta: the dog who charmed audiences in the six editions of the *Thin Man* movies. William Powell and Myrna Loy may have had top billing, but this terrier always stole the show.

Astro: the dog from the *Jetsons* television series.

Bagel: the beagle featured in much of the publicity for singer/songwriter Barry Manilow.

Balto: the great Siberian husky who pulled a sled filled with diphtheria serum in 1925 Alaska. His actions saved thousands of lives.

Bandit: the collie from *Little House on the Prairie.*

Barfy: the dog from the newspaper comic strip *Family Circus*.

Barry: the Saint Bernard responsible in the early 1800s for saving more than forty human lives in the Swiss Alps. He is the best-known rescue dog in the history of the canine world.

Beau: a golden retriever owned by Jimmy Stewart. He wrote best-selling poems about this dog who always ignored his calls.

Beethoven: the famed movie Saint Bernard.

Benji: the dog found by Frank Inn in an animal shelter and trained for stardom on *Petticoat Junction* and later in many movies.

Big Red: one of Hollywood's top dogs. This Irish setter was a big box-office draw in 1945, and his movie is still being sold on video today.

Billy: a London bulldog who made his living killing rats. Early in this century he was a rodent's worst nightmare.

Bimbo: the dog from the early *Betty Boop* cartoons.

Bingo: the dog on the Cracker Jack box.

Blackjack: the dog from the television series *Blansky's Beauties*.

Blanco: a white collie and one of Lyndon Johnson's personal pets. Blanco spent almost four years as Washington, D.C.'s top dog.

Bowser: the wolf-dog from the *Pistols 'N' Petticoats* TV series.

Bozo: the small mutt who was Jimmy Carter's childhood dog.

Brandi: one of Barbara Mandrell's two Saint Bernards. Tourists who stopped to take pictures of the country music singer's home were often greeted with wet, sloppy kisses by this giant canine.

Brutus: the Great Dane in the Disney movie *The Ugly Dachshund*.

Buck: a television star whose talent was overshadowed by his personality. Buck was a background player who always managed to attract the camera's attention on *Married . . . with Children*. Buck was also the name of a dog in Jack London's classic *Call of the Wild*.

Bud: the basketball-shooting golden retriever who starred in a movie, lost a leg to cancer, and kept on playing.

Buddy: the world's first Seeing Eye dog. Buddy first guided a blind master in the 1920s. Buddy was also what Bill Clinton named the First Dog, a chocolate Lab.

Bullet: Roy Rogers's dog. Most baby boomers will remember this German shepherd.

Bump: a dog that Rudd Weatherwax used in silent films.

Busy: one of George Washington's dogs.

Butkis: Rocky's dog in the movie series about the life of a boxer.

Cappuchine: Jeane Dixon's dog. It was claimed that she had psychic abilities.

Chance: the bulldog in the movie *Homeward Bound*.

Charley: writer John Steinbeck's poodle. He not only claimed this poodle as his best friend but took him on book tours and wrote a book called *Travels with Charley*.

Checkers: the cocker spaniel that almost ended then Vice President Richard Nixon's political career.

Cheffon: the real sheepdog in *The Shaggy Dog*, as opposed to the human who kept turning into a sheepdog.

Chief: one of the major players, a police dog, in *The Fox and the Hound*.

Chipper: the dog from the science fiction TV show *Land of the Giants*.

Chu Chu: fictional detective Charlie Chan's number one dog.

Cleo: the basset hound from the television classic *The People's Choice*.

Clifford: the giant dog of children's book fame.

Colin: a tricolored collie that helped start the breed's popularity in the United States. The dog began life as Queen Victoria's pet.

Comet: the golden retriever who appeared on *Full House*.

Copper: the hound in *The Fox and the Hound*.

Corky: the dog who costarred with Jackie Cooper in 1931's *The*

Champ. Rudd Weatherwax often called Corky the smartest dog he ever trained.

Daisy: the favorite dog in the *Blondie* comic strip and movie series. She was trained for the movies by Rudd Weatherwax.

Deputy Dawg: a cartoon dog who is a sheriff.

Dookie: the first of the British royal family's corgis. He was given to King George VI in 1933. The royal family still maintains corgis at Buckingham Palace.

Dot: Rutherford B. Hayes's spaniel.

Dreyfuss: He thought he was the most talented actor on *Empty Nest.* Some critics agreed.

Duke: the bloodhound that moved to Beverly Hills with television's Clampett family on *The Beverly Hillbillies.*

Earnest: newspaper columnist Dave Barry's favorite dog.

Eddie: the scene-stealing Jack Russell terrier on *Frazier.*

Fala: one of Franklin D. Roosevelt's dogs. This dog traveled all over the world with FDR and was featured in many newsreels and press photos.

Fang: the dog secret agent from television's *Get Smart.*

Fido: Many wonder where this name came from. History records that Abraham Lincoln named his dog Fido, and the mutt lived in the White House as long as his master.

Flash: the law's dog on *The Dukes of Hazzard.*

Fluke: the title character in the 1996 film.

Fred: the basset hound from the *Smokey and the Bandit* movies.

Freemont: George Wilson's dog on *Dennis the Menace.*

Freeway: the dog on the *Hart to Hart* television series.

Fugi: the dog on *The Osmonds* television show.

Gin Gin: Jeannie's dog on *I Dream of Jeannie.*

Goofy: the famous Disney hound.

Granite: This mixed breed led Susan Butcher's team in her 1986 victory in the world's most famous dog sled race, the Iditarod.

Gray Dawn: one of writer Albert Payson Terhune's best-loved collies.

Grayfriars Bobby: an English dog who guarded his dead master's grave for fourteen years until he died at his master's graveside. Lassie starred in the movie version of this story, *Challenge to Lassie*.

Grimm: The first famous Grim (spelled with a single "m") belonged to Rutherford B. Hayes. When most people hear this name now, they think of *Grimm's Fairy Tales* or the *Mother Goose and Grimm* comic strip.

Grits: the White House dog during Jimmy Carter's term in office.

Hank: John R. Erickson's cowdog in the mystery books that are the favorites of millions of children.

Happy: the Camdens' family dog on the television series *7th Heaven*.

Her: Along with Him, Her made up the beagle duo that moved to the White House with Lyndon and Lady Bird Johnson.

Hooch: the sloppy mastiff from the movie *Turner and Hooch*.

Hotdog: Jughead's dog in the *Archie* comics.

Huckleberry Hound: the famous slow-talking cartoon dog.

Hush Puppy: Shari Lewis's puppet dog.

Igloo: During the Depression this dog was almost as famous as his hero master, Admiral Byrd. While there is now debate whether Byrd was the first to reach the South Pole, there can be little argument that Igloo was the first dog to accomplish that feat.

Jack: the one-eyed terrier from the *Tales of the Gold Monkey* television series.

Jake: the talking golden retriever from the Bush beans commercial.

Jason: the basset hound mascot of Hush Puppies shoes.

Jasper: the family dog on the TV show *Bachelor Father*.

Jiggs: the U.S. Marine Corps' bulldog mascot.

189

King (or Yukon King): the dog on the TV series *Sergeant Preston of the Yukon.*

King Tut: a German shepherd who lived with Herbert Hoover in the White House. In those days life in Washington, D.C., was a bit simpler. This dog roamed the grounds at night to warn of intruders and fetched the paper for the president each morning. Who needs the Secret Service when King Tut is on the job?

Krypto: Superman's dog.

Lad: the name of writer Albert Payson Terhune's most famous dog and the name of the sheepdog from *Please Don't Eat the Daisies.* Lad was also the terrier's name in the television classic *Make Room for Daddy.*

Laddie: the most common traditional name for a male dog in Scotland.

Laddie Boy: He belonged to Warren G. Harding and was the only dog ever to have his own chair for cabinet meetings.

Laika: The first dog in space, Laika was launched into orbit on Sputnik 2 in 1957.

Lassie: What more need be said?

Liberty: Once the nation's best-known golden retriever, Liberty belonged to Gerald Ford.

Lord Nelson: Doris Day's dog on *The Doris Day Show.*

Lucky: the dog that Nancy Reagan kicked out of the White House for not behaving.

McGruff: Every child knows that he is the Crime Dog.

Marmaduke: the Great Dane who has been a comic strip and cartoon star for years.

Mathe: This greyhound is dogdom's best-known traitor. When King Richard was forced off the throne by brother Henry, this dog stayed with the new king rather than depart with his master.

Max: the bionic dog from the TV series *The Six Million Dollar Man.*

Meatball: the lead character's dog in the television series *Baa Baa Black Sheep.*

Melvin: Lassie's best friend in the 1990s. This Jack Russell terrier has appeared on many television episodes himself.

Millie: George and Barbara Bush's spaniel. Millie was the first dog to write a best-selling book.

Mr. Peabody: the incredibly smart dog from *Rocky and Bullwinkle.*

Murray: the dog on *Mad About You.*

Nanette: This German shepherd was Rin Tin Tin's sister.

Neil: the Saint Bernard from *Topper.*

Nick Carter: the world's most famous criminal-tracking bloodhound.

Nipper: the dog on RCA's trademark.

Odie: shares a home with the comic strip cat Garfield.

Old Yeller: the famous movie dog whose story brought tears to millions of theatergoers.

Otto: the uniform-wearing dog from the *Beetle Bailey* comic strip.

Petey: the *Our Gang* series dog; most famous for the circle around his eye.

Pilot: Mr. Rochester's dog in *Jane Eyre.*

Pluto: Mickey Mouse's pet dog.

Pokey: Jeff's best friend's dog on *Lassie.*

Pongo: the best-remembered dog from *101 Dalmatians.*

Prince: Barbie's poodle as well as the name of a dog from *Call of the Wild.*

Princess: the dog in the movie *Life with Father.*

Quark: the dog from *Honey I Shrunk the Kids.*

Rebel: the German shepherd on the *Adventures of Champion* television series of the 1950s.

Reckless: the dog on *The Waltons.*

Reveille: Texas A&M University's mascot, usually a collie.

Rex: the name given to many of literature's best-known dog companions.

Rin Tin Tin: The first "Rinty" began life as a World War I dog and was brought back to the States from France by U.S. troops. He first starred in silent films, and many German shepherds have taken up the role in motion pictures and television over the past seventy years.

Rob Roy: Calvin Coolidge's white collie.

Rover: The most famous owner of this name belonged to George Washington.

Rowlf: This dog plays piano for the Muppets.

Ruff: Dennis's dog in the *Dennis the Menace* comic strip. The character never appeared in the television show based on the strip.

Sam: the dog from the television series *Mr. Deeds Goes to Town;* also the name of the dog in *Hondo* (played by a Robert Weatherwax–trained Lassie double).

Sandy: the dog from *Little Orphan Annie.*

Scamp: Teddy Roosevelt's terrier.

Schotzie: the Saint Bernard who is the mascot for the Cincinnati Reds.

Scooby-Doo: a cartoon dog who solves mysteries with his human friends.

Shadow: the golden retriever in *Homeward Bound.*

Sharp: Queen Victoria's black Labrador.

Shep: a common name for a herding dog. Red Foley once had a hit recording that told the story of a dog named Ole Shep. At age fourteen, Elvis Presley sang the tearjerker at a county fair talent show and won first prize.

Simone: the *Partridge Family*'s dog.

Snert: the dog from the *Hagar the Horrible* comic strip.

Snoopy: the beagle who often imagines himself flying World War I planes in the *Peanuts* comic strip.

Snow-Job: the mutt who often traveled with his master, Bob Hope.

Sparky: the dalmatian who teaches kids about the dangers of fire.

Appendix: The Name Game

Spike: the bulldog who chased Tom in *Tom and Jerry*.

Spooch: the ghost-dog from *Casper*.

Spot: the dog from the *Dick and Jane* readers.

Spunky: Fonzie's dog on *Happy Days*.

Strongheart: A silent movie star and a former war hero, this German shepherd was filmdom's first great animal superstar.

Telek: one of Dwight D. Eisenhower's scotties.

Tige: the dog from the Buster Brown shoe ads.

Tiger: the *Brady Bunch* dog, and the name of the dog on TV's *Patty Duke Show*.

Timber Doodle: Charles Dickens's spaniel.

Toby: the criminal-tracking hound in the Sherlock Holmes adventures.

Toto: Dorothy's dog in *The Wizard of Oz*.

Tramp: the big, wonderful mutt from *My Three Sons*.

Tripoli: A Weatherwax family mutt gained fame playing this character in the movie *Air Force*.

Trusty: the bloodhound from *Lady and the Tramp*.

Underdog: the world's most famous superdog.

Vanilla: the name of the dog from the *Amos and Andy* radio show.

Veto: one of James Garfield's favorite dogs.

Waldo: the dog from the television series *Nanny and the Professor*.

Wegie: Herbert Hoover's German shepherd.

White Fang: the title character in the famous Jack London novel.

Wishbone: the PBS dog.

Wonderdog: the superdog from *Superfriends*.

Zeke: the cocker spaniel who lived in the Arkansas governor's mansion with Bill and Hillary Clinton.

Zeus: one of the Dobermans from *Magnum, P.I.*

Acknowledgments

I would like to thank the following people whose efforts made this book possible: Robert Weatherwax; Roy and Julie Young and the staff of the Young Animal Hospital in Hillsboro, Texas; and Cassie Jones, Gwen Petruska Gürkan, Lynda Castillo, and Anne Sullivan of Golden Books.

Thanks as well to the people who provided photographs for this book: Tommy Ally, Kathy Boltin, Valerie Bourron, Lynda and Bob Castillo, Kathryn Cox, Annie Kaufmann, Tracy Lefkowitz, the Leone family, Courtney Silk, and Robert Weatherwax.

Index

195

Index

Index

Index